MW01108443

LIFE IS A FOUR LETTER WORD

LIFE IS A FOUR LETTER WORD

FROM A CARE CENTER

CHARLENE COFFEY ALEXIS

Outskirts Press, Inc.
Denver, Colorado

Outskirts Press, Inc.
http://www.outskirtspress.com

ISBN: 978-1-4327-5268-2

Outskirts Press and the "OP" logo are trademarks belonging to Outskirts Press, Inc.

PRINTED IN THE UNITED STATES OF AMERICA

Dedication

To all the residents in all the care centers, nursing homes and assisted living facilities in the nation I dedicate these words of memory: Life, Love, Hope.

Persons depicted herein are not intended to be specific individuals per se, but in a true sense they represent each person here given certain situations. It is meant to show people with honor, respect, understanding and empathy due them as worthy individuals with frailties and strengths.

To their families and loved ones I encourage the recording of the life's stories of history, career, love, loss or events, for when they are gone, the stories, recipes and skills disappear. Listen, audio or video record, and/or write with your loved one. There is at least one story teller in each generation to step forward and capture the heritage events before they are gone.

In recognition of all the personal stories, memories, loves and skills and the happiness of all residents, I urge the involvement and encouragement of all activities directors of care centers to join in with such efforts.

And in honor of Metropolitan State College of Denver since August 18, 1965 for all the personal, student, faculty and administrative relationships and experiences which shaped much rich spiritual and intellectual growth. Additionally to all the Auraria experiences past, present and future I dedicate this work.

To my past and present extended Coffey family, the original ALEXIS SIX and all the grandchildren following and following.....

Proudly and humbly.....

Ila Charlene Coffey Alexis
Associate Professor Auraria Library retired. UCD

Table of Contents

Life Is a Four Letter Word

Mandatory naptime. She stretched out under a clean sheet resenting being forced into something and the wasted time it represented. She had been told it was good for her recovery process, but that did not promise wellness in any way.

Immediately she closed her eyes and remembered her Grandmother's introduction to her first born daughter, the new great granddaughter. She had meant to present her with such pride and joy, but instead the grandmother had said, "Oh, poor little thing, just think of all the pain and trials she will have to face!"

"But Grandma, just think of all the joy and happiness she will both give and get!" she had protested stroking the soft white blonde hair on top of her infant's head. All those years ago and the memories came back so clearly although she herself was now a grandmother in a care center!

Why was she remembering that now? Perhaps it was triggered by the scene she had come upon that morning as she left her room via wheelchair under her own steam. There sat a naked man in a wheelchair smack dab in the middle of the hallway in front of the nurses' station. A black leather belt snaked along the floor underneath. As she got closer she realized that the man had on a hospital gown which he pushed down into his lap. Rounding the corner she had come face to face with a woman sitting sound asleep in her wheelchair going the wrong way to have been headed for breakfast in the dining room.

Life is a four letter word. That was her immediate thought, but she smiled to realize, so is love, help, work, hope and, for that matter, soap. Today was her shower day. Having scribbled all her life, she could not give up that habit of thought. That would be a perfect title for a book now. LIFE IS A FOUR LETTER WORD. So many lives housed in this place, so many stories no one would ever write down, she thought with regret. Casual observation showed that it was a fortunate resident who had visitors.

The visitors she had were watched and questioned by other residents, hungry for some attention and something new to do. The many activities scheduled every day were not 24/7. Frequent visitors were warm and willing to share a smile and a touch. Staff responded to needs as they could. Some residents were noisy and cross, some smiling and pleasant, just people at their worst and best.

She could not stop the thought how much this place resembled a zoo, all the small cramped rooms with staff and visitors viewing performances of residents. The exception was that they brought with them little treasures, family photographs, flowers from well tended gardens, books, trinkets, stuffed toys and wreaths on the doors.

Scrambled eggs with cheese, cinnamon toast and a sausage patty were on the morning menu along with oatmeal, milk and orange juice. She had looked to the back of the dining room where her roommate sat among the other assisted residents who needed help with eating. She had been brought down by staff earlier.

Since scrambled eggs really meant powdered eggs, she always opted for boiled eggs, just to be sure hers were real, honest to goodness eggs. That came from having grown up on a farm with a flock of their own hens. One never strays far from her roots.

At breakfast one morning she overheard an 88 year old and a 78 year old compare notes on home butchering practices and longing for meat with each breakfast, especially crisp bacon. The elder of them grew up in a family with twelve children on a Kansas farm, the other from Oklahoma with five. Listening is a great skill.

Immediately thoughts went back to her roommate who was being assisted eating breakfast by a CNA among several others at the rear of the dining room along a bank of windows. The roommate was deaf, sometimes selectively so, and described herself as blind as a bat although she wore glasses with very thick lenses. She watched television at a blaring volume. Her visitors were almost non-existent. She was filled with gratitude for her own hearing and corrected sight, for her frequent visits from a caring family, for her career history, for her own computer and the somewhat friendly terms with which it treated her. Reading was a joyful use of time. It reinforced her conviction that when one stops learning she dies. What else would a librarian think? A touch on the shoulder and a warning --time for supper call made her realize that she had, in fact, fallen asleep during the mandatory nap time. The lift awaited her at bedside. It was into the wheelchair and off to the dining room shortly after the visit to the commode. Now she hoped the mandatory nap would not interfere with sleeping tonight. She braced herself and pushed up with her knees to answer the tug of the lift and its embracing belt across her back and under her arms. Although it meant a certain amount of pain, the stretch was a welcome change of position when she was lowered into the wheelchair.

Name

She made a game, almost a religious ritual, of learning names of residents and staff members alike. A light came on in the eyes when a resident heard her or his name called. She thought it was the proper reverse of identity theft, this giving of name recognition, acknowledgement of self. Why not? It was good mental exercise for her and gave meaning to personal contacts. So it was Mary, Maria, Bob, Larry, Bill, Dorothy, Peggy, Becky.. These names gave way to Tiffany, Tabitha, Alexandra, Stevie, Jackie, Juan, Raelyn, Katrina and Ruby, a generation's or two's difference on the CNA staff. There was a sprinkling of Marshas and Elizabeths and Teresas. It was a conversation with another resident which began her quest to learn names. Early on during her residency at the center when she ask a certain resident who another person was when she entered the dining room. "Nobody." was her answer. Automatically she gasped, "Nobody is NOBODY!" Everybody deserves their own name and recognition. She had to admit to being starved for male companionship since she had grown up the only girl with four younger brothers. Her husband had been gone for over twenty years now and her living brothers and uncle were out of state.

The center tended to seat all men at the table or all women in the dining room's assignments. Getting to know male residents presented a challenge. Her whole work career predominantly involved dealing with men, fellow administrators, deans, department chairpersons, professors, instructors. At first she was baffled by how she should handle the men with whom she worked. Finally she settled on the thought she should treat them as if they were her little brothers although most of them were older than she. Somehow it worked and she enjoyed the exchanges.

Most of the male residents at the center seemed to seek identity in the head gear they wore: a Broncos ball cap, a safari guide's hat with wide brim and chin strap, a natural colored straw hat finished off with brown or white cotton work gloves. One 85 year old wore a ball cap with company logo. He had struck up a conversation about his electrical business and growing up on the beaches of the North Carolina coast. His current interest was a flock of tiny dark birds which frequented the tree top just outside the glass emergency exit doors at the end of the hallway. He was puzzled about the kind of birds and when they would fly south. He was interesting to talk with and shared a room with another gentleman not too far down the hall. She and one of his granddaughters shared a given name. He was pleasant and a favorite of the staff because of his friendly and cooperative attitude.

She shared that her farmer grandfather had been born in North Carolina, on the far western end near Tennessee, but had settled in Oklahoma Territory in 1899 during the Cheyenne Arapahoe land opening. Geography lessons shared!

She teased the activities' staff that she could write a novel about what she observed at the center, but that she figured she'd get her pants sued off. That is why she wrote using no names for herself or the cast of characters. Just for fun she volunteered to be a resident editor of the center's newsletter. There names were permitted, demanded. Names play tricks on the mind, for just when she thought she knew a person's ethnic origin, an Ellis

Island hatchet job proved her guess wrong. Besides most residents are women. Women marry and change their names. Then when she thought of the very long original spelling of her Irish maiden name, she realized that how ever pleasant and intriguing her name, there was room for error. Once she met the wife of an administrator, named Antoinette Mc Entire who surprised her by being Chinese. Her parents were originally from Hong Kong when it had French Indo China influence and she was married to a Scot-Irish man. So much for jumping to conclusions!

She remembered with a chuckle the story told her by a teacher who shared her Irish maiden name. His forbearers were actually O'Coffeys who came to America because of the potato famine to work on the railroad. They thought they were so smart when they discovered they were hiring in alphabetical order and had that morning become the Coffeys. Then they discovered just ahead of them in line the Caseys who until that morning had been the O'Caseys. Just for fun when memory failed her, residents were given secret nicknames such as Squeaky and "the Whistler" or "the Roamer", and there were many roamers. They just entered any room chosen, without invitation and for their own reasons. "Can I use your potty?" "No, yours is right down the hall." There were those who could not remember their room numbers or how to get to their own room. They remembered their name and resisted being unrecognized by name and place in the dining room.

One very deaf person is also a roamer. She came uninvited, unannounced into her neighbor's room while she was reading and watching television at the same time as she often did. Suddenly, silently, there was this little gray haired person in a wheelchair in the middle of her private room headed for her service table. She said, "This isn't your room. Your room is down the hall." No response. The eager hand reached out to find the banana which awaited the resident for her after-morning-meds snack. She opened her mouth to say No and turned on the call light to alert staff about her visitor. No response. The visitor bit the end off the banana and happily gulped away. "Well, okay, if you are that hungry, go ahead!" No response and no name to call her--if she could hear. Staff to the rescue and they wheeled her back in the direction of the proper room. "She got by us!" was their response. "Do you want a banana from the kitchen?" "No, that's okay." No name. Then she sorted through her own writings about family to locate the short essay about her grandfathers: George Grant Walker born 1/5/1865 and Austin Julian Coffey born 1/6/1878. Both were remembered and treasured family names.

REMEMBER*****PINK MINTS AND LEMON DROPS

Grandpa Walker lived up to his name. Sometimes when he would allow company on his walks, he would hand me a pink mint candy circle. He could make his mint last forever and I knew he would not offer me another until he had finished his. I always managed to bite mine. It melted quickly. He was famous for saying, "If you are going to walk, WALK. If we are going to talk, TALK." That was his way of saying politely, "Be quiet and don't bother my thoughts." He really only talked to my Daddy when they argued philosophy and politics. They never ventured into religion, for some reason. These were two dryland farmers who read everything they got their hands on. He really only spoke to his daughter, my Mother, briefly when he wanted some hot tea or something. The five of us kids knew that we were to be quiet when Grandpa Walker came to visit.

Once Grandma Walker died Grandpa just went from one to the other of his nine remaining children and rented out his farm to a daughter's family. One daughter had died of the flu at the age of 19 leaving a year old daughter. I was a listener. That was the only role a child, a girl at that, was allowed at the time. But I did learn many things and when he divided up his household things he some how recognized a future librarian in his midst. He gave me all his books, including Thomas Carlyle's multi-volume

FREDERICK THE GREAT. Pink mints last longer than one would think.

Grand-dad Coffey, thirteen years younger almost to the day than Grandpa Walker, was a wiry, hard working farmer who filed on land in the Cheyenne-Arapahoe opening in Oklahoma Territory in 1899. He was orphaned early in his native North Carolina and had come as a teen to Texas and then to the Chickasaw Nation where he got a work permit as a day laborer in the 1890's. After the Civil War, Chickasaw citizens replaced slave laborers with white tenant farmers and young white day laborers. When I was little, Grand-dad Coffey often offered me some of his lemon drops which were sometimes covered with lint or dried cotton leaves which found their ways into his overalls pockets. The whole family pulled cotton on his land or for neighbors in the area to earn money for school clothes, a new oil cloth for the kitchen table, sacks of pinto beans or a big box of oatmeal. He always raised chickens, too, so even during the really grueling, desperate days of the dust bowl, we had something good to eat, but less when the crops did not make.

Both he and Daddy worked hard and since Grand-dad owned (or it owned him) a piece of land we perched on the corner of that place and farmed together. That red dirt saved us from becoming Okies who fled to California. Because he was orphaned early, I doubt that he went to school much beyond the fourth grade, if that, but he was smart in his own way. (It was Grandma who was the reader in that family.) But he could figure quickly in his head and was honest in his dealings. He never asked any of his sons or his one daughter to do anything without being right there involved in the work beside them. The lemon drops he shared readily with me and with my four brothers whenever he had the money to buy them. He had a weakness for homemade French vanilla custard ice cream which we often had on the 4th of July. He listened to us kids and laughed with us, a quiet almost silent laugh which came from way down deep somewhere. He was a quiet teetotaler who lived every inch of his Baptist beliefs and he lived up to the meaning of his surname. Coffey is an Irish name which means Victorious. I doubt he ever knew that fact, but he lived that every day also. (What I did not know then was that his late father had been a North Carolina moon shiner which sealed his fate to be a teetotaler when his older brother was a wild sort of preacher and his youngest brother was a drinker. (So much for genes!) When he shook hands with Daddy agreeing to sell him the home place in 1953, Daddy asked him whether he could use some cash money right then upfront. Grand-dad said, "Yeah, I reckon I could." It was only then that he showed Daddy his bank book. The balance was exactly zero. Daddy said to Mother, "I never would have known if I hadn't asked to buy the place that they had been living on cream and egg money all that time." Of course, that was often the case with dryland farmers in Southwestern Oklahoma. Hard, sweet, and sour lemon drops spoke volumes.

She thought sweet memories. "We are a part of every person we have ever known. That goes at least double for family. I am thankful for my pink mint and lemon drop heritage." With quiet gratitude she smoothed the pages before her, remembering that all of the five kids, she and her four brothers, each one earned at least one college degree and some earned two. Work is a four letter word and a victorious name helped. Daddy always said the most valuable thing a man has to offer is his own good name.

CNAs

She learned that there is something CNAs (Certified Nursing Assistants) can not do. They can not do six things at once. She had seen them run their legs off answering call lights and cries for help when she is all alone with her back up on meal break or answering another call light. They are lowest on the totem pole in the eyes of some, but she stood by her declaration and challenge made to a small group of new hires. All happened to be CNAs when she was asked by the staff development office to speak on the subject of what it was like being a resident in the care center. "In my eyes CNAs run the place," she said. "Because you answer my call light when I am in need!"

She wanted to go on to say this is our current home, not by choice but by necessity. We have to depend on you to dress us, get us to the toilet, to put us to bed and get us up each morning and to see that we get to the dining room or are otherwise fed. You are our lifeline, our companions. It takes a special kind of person to do your job well. Not everyone succeeds, but most of you try. "If and when you are not treated with the respect you are due, I apologize for the offenders' ignorance. When you meet our needs and even exceed our expectations, I thank you. In my own career I have recruited and supervised many people in another profession, but I know people who work well together and who goofs off and who will knife-others in the back to build themselves up in the eyes of upper staff. I also know those of you who work your tail-feathers off and who dodges duty. I also know who among the upper echelon of staffing succumb to putting you down if not in front of others in their own attitude. I wish I were in a position to right all wrongs, but I am not. We will just have to settle for my doing what I can when I can. The excellent ones among you call everyone by name, touch the backs of those nearby when they go through the crowded dining room and are quick to bring coffee to residents as appropriate without even being asked because you know each one and their preferences. They know when pain and mental lapses come across as harsh and demanding without cause." This later part she could not and did not say in the class of CNAs, but she wanted to do so. CNAs are not saints, but some are candidates for nomination.

One night she was especially tired of sitting in her wheelchair and a very young CNA came in to check on her call light and learned of her need for a lift. She came in much, much later very apologetic for the delay. The resident asked whether they were short staffed and was told "No." Then she asked who was on duty only to learn five names plus the nurse at the station. She recognized two of the group to be experienced staff members, but slow goof-offs and another to be a new slow moving individual. The experienced ones were not noted for team work when they did work. This young and new CNA was carrying the whole load for the wing while experiencing a dinging headache. She had asked her how she was earlier. She confided that it is her upbringing. "You always carry your share of the load." She saw that she complimented the young CNA to the nurse in charge after she complimented the CNA directly. She considered reporting her experiences to the head nurse. One of the experienced CNA's had come in her room while she was on the commode and asked are you about through. (Another CNA was assigned to her and this CNA was just trying to grab the lift right off her.) She had said "No." emphatically and loudly. She had on another day come in when she was back-up to another staff member, turned off the call light and informed her she'd have to wait for her own CNA without even asking what was needed. Bad form, bad attitude, she had just turned her light right back on, for she had not done anything nor had she even tried to determine what the need really was. That CNA brown-noses the nurses at every turn, so the resident automatically expects nothing from her, or worse. Gall.

There is a thin line between friendship and patient/caregiver relationships. Each seeing the other as individual human beings is essential; it is even healing. A tight rope, a balancing act! Unless the CNAs and nurses truly care, good treatment is impossible. Every resident has to decide what caring level means and is comfortable, she decided. Certain of the staff needed and was awarded a caring relationship from her. Others were not meant to be that close. Her own supervisory experiences tend to label goof-offs and those who have real skills or potentials. A caring attitude helps immeasurably. She tries to limit demands upon staff, so she automatically expects performance when she does call. She tries to assess personality traits and weigh them against her own. One CNA told her "I am so glad you have a sense of humor so I can tease a bit. It makes the day go better than when someone is always sour." Respect and an occasional display of good humor is the key to good relations all the way round.

CNAs have the hardest and most crucial job in the whole place.

Moon

An aide rushed in breathlessly. "There has to be a full moon out there." She muttered quietly under her breath. Noises and commotions were audible down the hallways as people were scurrying to settle in for the night. She knew full well it was a hectic night and what the aide meant, but the moon meant a totally different thing to her. Hurriedly she was made ready for bed and tucked in. The remark had triggered a wealth of memories, thoughts of long ago. She was out on the front porch with various family members eating a glass of cornbread and milk which was a ritual when she spent nights with her grandparents. Everyone enjoyed the cornbread and watched the moon come up. Invariably her uncle would remind everyone of her stunt when about two; she had cried and danced reaching up saying, "Moon, Moon! I want it!" When they asked her what she was going to do with it, her answer had been, "I want to bounce the big ball!" She would just as invariably say "Ah, no, sirrree. I didn't do that!" He'd say, "There is no end of things you did, Kid!" Being the first born grandchild on the Coffey side of the family was a warm wonderful role to play.

The moon took on new meaning when her brother next in line to her became involved in the space program. From Great Falls, to Cocoa Beach (now Cape Canevaral) to the Jet Propulsion Labs, the family followed him and his career in space engineering, via CBS and Walter Cronkite's reports along with family letters. She was astounded at the thought "This is the kid whose geometry problems I solved and whom I despaired would ever graduate from high school!" Oh, he understood math full well; he was just more interested in girls and other things. He was conning his big sister. To think that one teacher could make such a difference for one student.

Physics was offered for the first time in the rural high school and the topic took on a decided electronic flavor. The kid was hooked. He also had ideas and gifts of his own such as building an over the tractor umbrella when there were no tractors with factory made ones or cabs attached. His tractor also had a radio which alarmed and sparked much curiosity along the country roads near their fields. Lots of necks were craned trying to locate the source of country music and hymns floating across the farmscape. When a former co-worker was frustrated with lack of progress on a project at the Jet Propulsion Lab, he plead with his supervisor, "Get me, Coffey. He will know what I am talking about." Thus he triggered a move from Florida to California. Those two made quite a team. When there was an opportunity for a consultation between JPL and Martin Marietta in the Denver area, the two of them came to visit his sister in Aurora. Her brother was eager to explain to her how they intended to use the gravity of a planet to swing a satellite around it and do loop-de-loops among the planets. That is a pretty good application of geometry with a purpose!

When her brother died of cancer at the age of 47, he had ask his wife to have his memorial service in their big old church. He said, "That is the only way I can get some of those guys to come to church with me." His two daughters became doctors, one told her, "My kids ask me about Daddy, the grandfather they could not know, and there is just so much I don't know about him." Although she had written VICTORIOUS about her family growing up in Oklahoma during the dust bowl and great depression days, she had written a long character sketch entitled "Lyndall." and had snapshots copied for the two daughters in honor of a truly moon and star struck father from a perspective they could not know.

It was with great excitement that she read about and then saw the movie, OCTOBER SKY. It was based on the book ROCKET BOYS about a West Virginia kid who had a gifted teacher who died young and how he and some classmates made and experimented with rockets. He wound up at NASA. There is always the moon and Mars, the sky's the limit! Or is it?

"Shoot for the moon!" "Reach for the stars!" These encouragements found their ways into the family conversations sometimes. It was meant to build a personal passion in each child's mind and heart. It was not meant against anyone else, but for themselves.

The brothers had teased her that she had always ruined things for them. Because she made good grades, it was expected that they follow. She protested "Daddy just says we should do the best we possibly can. That's all!"

Uncle Ivan had run away from home. For years he lived in California. When her four brothers were out of school they decided to go to California on a trip to visit him and two aunts on the Walker side of the family. He dreaded meeting those boys, even seeing them, but when they had come briefly and had gone, he had called the eldest of his sisters to say, "I have never been so thoroughly spanked for my judgments. Those are four of the nicest, most solid young men I have ever met." Here he had thought that the only possible reason they could have for coming to see them was to hit him up for money. "Daddy just says we should do the best we possibly can. That's all!"

Her father did not own a square inch of land until she went away to graduate school, but he bought War Bonds--Savings Bonds with the income from the crops until he could pay cash for the home place. It was with the family sweat and effort that this was possible. Shoot for the moon! With determination it isn't always that far away. Progress is a matter of inches and determination. Her brothers knew that and she did, too. They learned it from parents and grandparents and each other. The full moon may drive some crazy, but others it inspires. She smiled and fell into a peaceful sleep. She awoke remembering her then 6 year old granddaughter in the "mutton bustin" contest at the National Western Stock Show in Denver. She had rode and rode and rode well past the expected time limit in the contest. An official came up to the side of the lamb and asked whether she wanted help off the poor little beast. She told him, "No. I want to win!" And she did. The moon isn't always that far away!

Time

"You Are My Sunshine." followed by "I Saw The Light" began the mini-concert before church that first Sunday morning of day light savings time. Those present were a little droopy eyed at the beginning of the service since they had just missed an hour of sleep. Time hangs heavily on some of the residents who have few and infrequent visitors and have not signed on to a schedule of activities of their choice. She remembered asking her Grandmother to tell her about the days of coming from Texas to Oklahoma Territory to file on newly opened acreages which would eventually become the southwestern portion of the state. She wondered whether it seemed like a long time ago to her. The answer was "Yes and no, some times it seems like forever ago and some times it seems like yesterday!" Now she understood what the grandmother meant.

Discussions during Story Hour, Good Old Days and often at the dining table, reflected those feelings. .One morning at the breakfast table an aide complimented a resident's perky striped blouse. That was met with a shy smile and comment that it was 25 years old and someone had stolen the bow that belonged at the neck, but she liked it a lot. She commented that it had cost her $10. It was the first time the observer had seen her wear it. Everything old is new again?

With a bemused smile she remembered celebrating her birthday with her four year old observing her frosting the cake. The daughter asked her how old she was. Hearing the answer of 34 the four year old gasped, "Mommy, is that the last number?" She had said, "If that is the last number how do you have a living grandmother and a living great-grandmother!" The child's eyes widened and she responded in awe, "Oh!" Time flies and it never stands still. She smiled at the thought of how much her memories resembled a row of dominoes which tumbled this way and that on a whim.

Once she informed her own mother that it wasn't her birthdays that impressed her, it was her younger brothers' ages kicking her up the hill! To which her mother replied, "What do you think you do to me!" Then she caught her breath in the realization that the cluster of April birthdays--her own, her son's and her granddaughter's ages--totals were impressive! She could not help gasping to herself, "When did all that happen? Where does time go? "

Political campaigns and elections demand comparisons and questions from young staff members about "Is this economic crisis like the Great Depression? Was FDR really a good president? Obama seems to praise his policies. What do you think?" We have lived and are living history. "We all have experiences which need to be shared. When we are gone those stories are gone," she thought and shared that opinion when asked. She encouraged fellow residents to write or have family members write for them their life history. Family members need to understand who they are, the heritage they share. Time, both past and present, is precious. Every time a new SPENDING proposal came up in a news report she was immediately reminded of the mandate from FDR and Henry A. Wallace, Secretary of Agriculture at the time. "Plow up every third row of cotton." Those were their words of wisdom meant to solve the surplus of cotton which made the price per pound lower. There was no thought that farmers had already borrowed money for tractor gas and cotton seed to put in that crop (not to mention time and sweat spent).

It had prompted her to ask her father at age 6 how they expected him to plow up every third row with a two row tractor. He answered that two out of six would have to do. But cotton was their only money crop supplemented by cream and egg money to eke by on a very tight to zero budget.

Just whose side was the government on she had wondered. The Good Lord had the last word. It just did not rain, so there was no cotton crop to gather that year. She saw that experience as her childhood introduction to politics and economics. The depression was doubled by the dust bowl. The truth was that her neck of the woods did not experience recovery until World War II jolted the economy into action. He was elected for four terms, so he ought to get some things right. That isn't to say that nothing FDR accomplished was worth while. It all depends upon the passage of time and which end of the telescope you are looking through. She remembered one of her very favorite teachers telling the high school science class that if it had not been for the Civilian Conservation Corps he would have starved to death because his parents simply could not feed their whole big family during the depression and the dust bowl. The young men were fed and housed for their labors and the family was sent $25 a month for their son's time and effort. He then went into the army and earned his teaching degree at Southwestern courtesy of the G. I. Bill.

Respecting time and history is important. She remembered a children's book on Native American culture called CROW AND WEASEL by Barry Lopez which stated: "Remember only this one thing....the stories people tell have a way of taking care of them. If stories come to you, care for them, and learn to give them away where they are needed. Sometimes a person needs a story more than food to stay alive. That is why we put these stories in each other's memory. This is how people care for themselves."

Sitting holding her hands for endless hours, whistling under his breath and tapping his foot in frustration, stroking and kissing the long soft ears of a stuffed animal for company and comfort--these to make time pass until an aide comes to remind them of meals or an activity going on in the lobby. Others roam endlessly up and down the halls and entering someone's room uninvited at times. That is how important visitors and planned events are. .She wondered whether those observed doing nothing were also the ones who had pestered their mothers with whining "Mama, what can I do now?" or "Mama, I am bored." As a child, "Find something to do or I'll think up a chore for you." had been her mother's answer. These days she found many things to do to entertain herself such as reading or writing and watching television, to participate or not participate in an activity was her choice. She wondered with a gasp. "Oh, what if I were blind!" How does a blind person deal with time? Oh, talking books!

Alexander Pope, the English poet, was right. " 'Tis with our judgments as with our watches. All differ, but each believes his own."

A high school teacher sent one of his students to her to be a resource on the topic of the dust bowl days and the current environment. She had asked some very deep and penetrating questions. As they were finishing the discussion the teen-ager tilted her head and looked at her curiously. "I read about all this in black and white. But you see it in COLOR!"

Living for a long time has its benefits. Longevity does not guarantee wisdom, but it at least adds dimension

Race

Or should it be ethnicity? She could not address the subject of race without thinking of Joe Louis, the boxing champion. There were maybe two or three Negroes (the proper term during her childhood days) in the county seat town, but the radio broadcasts of the boxing matches fascinated her. She was a big overgrown girl in rural Oklahoma and was headed for the Saturday matinee with some cotton-chopping money in hand when a little sawed-off old man approached her on the street. She was dressed in a two piece suit her Mother had made and feeling pretty proud of herself, but she was a country kid. She was not to talk to strangers on the street. "Boy!" he declared looking her up and down, "If you had been in that ring the other night, you'd have showed that _____(N word) a thing or two!" She did not know this man from Adam and she was startled that he had the gall to speak to her let alone by what he said.

She decided to break the rules and tell him what for. "Oh, no, sir, I wouldn't have hurt the poor man for anything. I am sort of sentimental about heroes." He picked his chin up off the sidewalk, turned on his heel and walked away. She did not know where her words had come from. It certainly was not from first hand knowl-edge. It seemed that people should allow a person to be just that, a person, without skin searing judgment.

Later she found a tattered copy of the autobiography of Joe Louis in the school library and read it. She was surprised to find a passage in the book which read "All Negroes are Baptist or somebody has been meddling!" That's the craziest thing she ever heard of. Then she asked herself, "If you are so smart, why are you Baptist?" She read her Bible and what she could get her hands on and considered whether she was Baptist because that was honest-ly what she thought or just because her parents and grandparents were. After long consideration she came back pretty much to where she started only with deeper convictions. Labels are tricky, but given the independent thinking and democratic governance of the Baptist Churches she knew, she understood why Joe Louis could make that statement.

In the third grade the teacher had given a rousing lesson in geography and the different races of people on the earth. She came home excited and wanting to ask her beloved grandmother about her beautiful dark complexion, bright brown eyes and her long black braid. "Grandma, are you an Indian or Mexican or something?" She thought she was going to slap her and she was the first born grandchild, the golden child! She never did learn whether there was Indian blood in her lineage. She did not know enough about history and anthropology at the time to realize that Mexicans are far more "Native American" than Spanish. Race is a sore subject at times.

The book and movie SOUNDER, about a little African American boy searching for his father who was jailed for stealing a ham to feed the family, was a learning experience for her. She was a room mother who rode the school bus to the theater with the 5th and 6th graders which included her daughter. She asked her daughter's seatmate whether she could picture her Dad as that little boy, for she knew he had grown up in the Carolinas in a rural area much like the movie portrayed. She smiled at the contrast and comparison of her daughter with her platinum blonde pigtails and her friend's long black braids, next door neighbor girls, classmates. When she said she could not picture her Dad as that character, the answer had been "No." Then she realized that the Dad the girl saw was a sergeant in the military who took their family to England and Germany, all sorts of places where he was stationed. She had thought to herself, my kids are going to know who they are, their heritage.

A couple of weeks later, her daughter said to her, "Mom, you tell me you used to pull cotton and hoe cotton when you were a kid. And I don't understand, I thought only poor share croppers did that." She asked her what she thought her Grandfather was then, a tenant farmer, a share cropper. She repeated, "but I don't understand."

It was then it dawned on her that she thought all share croppers were black. When she shared this all with a fellow faculty member and friend who was an African American economics professor from South Carolina, he asked, "Where would she get a fool notion like that?"

She had smiled and said, "Now, Earl, be fair! In every textbook what do all the illustrations show, African Americans picking cotton in baskets, not pulling cotton in sacks and not a white face in the bunch!"

He drew his breath and chuckled, "We just can't get nothing right, can we?" She was pleased that he understood. They both laughed.

A Hispanic woman was assigned as one of her tablemates. She rarely spoke even to the Spanish speaking aides. Gradually she became aware when she gave her a certain look that she expected her to say "Two soft fried eggs, toast and orange juice" for her. Once she surprised her by saying, "No, French toast!"

She had laughed and said, "You fooled me!" They both laughed.

When her granddaughter who was having a hard time deal-ing with the fact her grandmother was unable to return to her own apartment, heard this, she said, "Oh, that's why God has you there. To speak for her!"

When she was a young teen she was fascinated by two Cheyenne Indian men with their colorful braids and blankets who always sat on the sidewalk observing and being observed in front of the bus station in the county seat town. She wanted desper-ately just to sit down with them against the brick wall flat on the concrete and learn everything about their lives, their homes and children. Had they attended Red Moon School or Ft. Sill School? What went on inside their heads and homes, but obviously she did not speak to them? All she could do was read whatever she could get her hands on.

She went back in memory to a concert in the college audito-rium featuring a very gifted Negro quartet and their accompanist. She had been so enthralled, for it was a great and enjoyable experience. She was shocked when she went to work in the caf-eteria and saw that they had served them in the usual area for guests, but there were no table linens or any thing special guests were usually afforded. When she gave an enthusiastic review of their performance to a fellow student he had snarled, "All I saw was a bunch of ---N word!" What in the world was going on? Judgmental bias and bitter views! She wondered where her own attitude came from as well as that of her fellow student. This was the summer of 1949 and her supervisor, manager of the cafeteria, was an ex-WAC. Her Mother would have said, "Other people's children!"

Her junior high daughter had come home reporting that a group of African American girls had been giving her a bad time at school--bullying and name calling. She had got mad and called them the N word. Up walked her next door neighbor friend who was also an African American and they challenged her to call her what she was. She said, "Okay, I will." She said warmly, "Hello,

Neighbor!" Then she added, "I call people what they act like." and walked away. That ended that.

Two Hispanic professors --friends and fellow faculty members came to mind. One was originally from Cuba and a personal acquaintance of Castro. He had just become the head of the Modern Language Department. In the first faculty meeting he proudly listed all the curricular offerings of the department and suddenly his expression and tone changed when he said, "And if you want to learn Russian, go to Cuba!" It was said with such sadness and suppressed anger that the room was electrified. The issue was recent, raw. He had left large land holdings in Cuba to come to the U. S. with a wife and 5 children, one a newborn baby. He had $100. in his pocket and the challenge to start all over.

Some time later he had come into her office to ask what she thought about reading the Bible. Then he said that he felt an urgency to do so. Before he started to leave he asked, "Do you think that God is telling me I am going to die?" Smiling she had handed him a copy of GOOD NEWS FOR MODERN MAN. It was a recent release of a modern English version of the NEW TESTAMENT. "I think God is saying you're just beginning to live."

The other professor had worked his way through a doctorate and on to a good administrative career at the college. He came by her office to tell her that he was so disappointed that he had worked so hard to buy a big home in the Cherry Creek school district for his kids' sake. Then he discovered that they were attending school with a bunch of rural types, farm kids. Obviously he did not know her early background. She swallowed a giggle and said, "Isn't that wonderful! Think of all the diversity in education your kids get for free!" His field was sociology and he was creator and publisher of the Spanish language magazine La Luz. He sputtered and grinned as he left. At the end of their acquaintance he stopped by the reference desk to tell her he had been diagnosed with terminal cancer. Friends are friends. Ethnicity has nothing to do with it.

It was then she remembered a librarian's application for a cataloger's position. She presented a letter with erasures and a smudge. She brought it by her office in person without an appointment. Her Phillipino accent made her difficult to be understand at first. As she discussed her professional experience and her family information started to make an impact on her. She thanked her and indicated that there were several other candidates. Then she heard her parting remark, "I'll go home and pray about it and we'll see."

She had no way of knowing that would strike a cord with her; further she realized that her family with five young children had just arrived in the U. S. and she was already working in a clerical position to help support her family. Once she was on faculty she more than proved her worth. Because she had three daughters as did her supervisor, it was natural that she offer to pass out-grown clothes on to a new family. When another staff member called her aside to say, "Don't you realize that she is shaming you?"

Her response was, "No, she is not. She loves me!" As a child she had lived through Japanese occupation and experienced seeing General Douglas Mac Arthur's promise, "I shall return" become a reality. It would be hard to judge who was more a blessing to whom.

Not to be forgotten was a fellow Oklahoman and fellow Baptist, a Cherokee, on faculty. He was tall, handsome and gentle. He was a world wide traveler and an eloquent talker who shared his slides and adventures with her Baptist Student Union. One student had come into a presentation late and did not hear the locale being discussed. He got so excited and said aloud. "I played right there by that huge rock. My parents were missionaries there!" Those two had quite a chat after the presentation. Later her Cherokee friend confided about his childhood, "You've never been hit in your life until you have been socked by a 6 foot 4 inch Cherokee." He was a collector and a generous sharer of experiences in the Middle East during the reign of the Shah in Iran. He told of having to evacuate and head back home. Dutifully he packed his belongings for shipment to the U. S. He did not dare implicate any Iranian citizen in this process, so he enlisted the aid of a Lebanese Christian friend to send his possessions back to the U.S. When they got to N. Y. they were opened and pillaged! She had a good discussion on the subject of trust triggered by this experience.

At the risk of being considered simplistic, she summed up her personal views of sociology in spite of assessing all the scholarly works she had ever read, by reviewing a children's chorus. "Jesus loves the little children, all the children of the world. Red and yellow, black and white, they are precious in His sight. Jesus loves the little children of the world." Then for good measure she threw in Dr. Suess' thoughts about star bellied Sneetches. Discernment decides on friends, true friends. She clung to her own favorite assessment: "You can slap any label on any old bottle, but it's what's on the inside that counts!"

Obviously, not all members of any one race are trustworthy, but open-mindedness seemed preferable. Don't judge, for those who are in the wrong will hang themselves eventually.

To her surprise she rediscovered a draft of her high school graduation address delivered May of 1948 in Sweetwater High School, Beckham County in southwestern Oklahoma.. It is always both a surprise and an affirmation of convictions long held and lived by. She smoothed out the two pages of notes hand written on scalloped edged pink stationery with loving memories and read:

Dear Friends, one and all,
The class of 1948 extends to you a most cordial welcome. We have met together on this momentous occasion to receive our diplomas. The seniors are indeed grateful to our friends and relatives who have made our education possible. We realize that the greatest education of all lies before us, that experience of dealing fairly with our fellowmen. As seniors of

today we have the tremendous responsibility of being not only Oklahomans and Americans, but world citizens, for the globe has diminished considerably in the past quarter of a century.

It is paramount that we know full well the importance of a tolerant attitude toward all men. That every man wrong or right has as firm a belief in his ideals as you and I do in ours; therefore everyone has the right to his own opinion. As world citizens we should respect all men--black, yellow, brown, red or white--who are worthy of respect. It was Lincoln who said, "I will walk by the man who is right, stay by him while he is right, but depart from him when he goes wrong."

We naturally believe that our democratic form of government is the best the world knows or ever will know, but there are nations, one particularly strong nation whose beliefs in government and religion are world's apart from ours. Our leaders and theirs may think differently, but the salt of the earth, the common men are very nearly the same all over the world, they love peace, want to live and rear families and are willing to treat anyone fairly who will deal fairly with them.

For many years famous thinkers and statesmen have dreamed, hoped, worked and prayed for a great world-wide brotherhood of nations, and this dream can become a reality if men will practice a policy of give and take. That is the way fellowship between countries should be, willing to compromise when good things are being considered, but never compromising with wrong.

You may think me a foolish young idealist. Youngsters see the world through rose-colored glasses. Perhaps, but if growing old means losing faith in my fellowman, then, please, God, keep me young! THE END.

How far had she come in thought and conviction over the years? She wasn't at all sure what shaped her stance. It wasn't politics

Salt

Brittle teeth and yet another major chipping away of enamel from a molar, forced her to consider total extraction and dentures. That added to a sore gum and a swollen lower jaw and threat of major infection settled the issue. A bitter little memory crept into her mind. "Thanks a lot Billy Landtroop!" Waiting for a hayride to start, teens gathered in and around the church building for the tractor driver to arrive with the hay wagon to take the group on their party hayride. The love of showing off, prompted Billy to throw a rock into the small country church building. It struck her square in the mouth. Her upper lip saved her from the breaking of her front tooth, but damage was done. It was not until years later that the dentist declared that a blow had killed that tooth and that it called for a root canal and replacement of her left front tooth. That was the first real problem, but wear and tear called for numerous fillings and extractions over the years.

She saw a dentist and was also referred to an oral surgeon. She both looked forward to and dreaded the date's arrival. During the surgery removing the remaining teeth, her constant thought was the Biblical promise: "Thou will keep him in perfect peace whose mind is stayed on Thee." It helped immeasurably throughout the two hour procedure. True grit was demanded during recovery from bruised and swollen chin and jaws in addition to wounded and stitched gums. It was a long and painful healing process which required ounces of numerous swishes of strong salt water several times a day. Waiting for the effects of the blood thinning meds corrected the blood flow, but the remaining effect in facial tissues caused major bruising. Nurses joked that she looked as if she had been in a 13 round boxing match and lost. Numerous liquid and/ or soft meals to adjust and follow-up appointments to both the dentist and oral surgeon were required.

Ceasing Physical Therapy's progress to concentrate all her energies for a week on healing was recommended. Reward for the resting was followed by the ability to use the walker for a 30 foot stretch after the first resumption of Physical Therapy sessions. This performance was a surprise to the therapist and the resident, for it topped her previous record by 5 feet. .Little steps of progress prepare the way for the months of recovery and healing which still remain.

"It's like pulling teeth," is not an idle saying! Having forethought and wisdom in choosing a very good dentist and an excellent oral surgeon who work well together is highly recommended! In a teasing mood after a painful denture removal and cleaning session, she had said to a favorite CNA, "I have promised myself that I'll never go through this surgery again!" Sharing a senseless laugh helps both parties. She thought that she must remember during the next care conference to suggest emphasis on training to encourage better oral care skills for some of the CNAs who seem to be reluctant to devote time to this process. Some were squeamish, some are inept, some were just reluctant to cause potential pain. Others just seemed to grasp what needed to be done and did it. All she cared about was cleanliness along with removal and replacement of dentures in a PAINLESS fashion. Yes, and lots of soothing salt water rinses!

Ears

He that hath an ear let him hear. That warning appears several places in The Holy Bible. She was reading a book about an experimental program on writing poetry in an east coast nursing home before she went to bed the night before. When she got down to breakfast this was what she heard.

SURPRISE

"Tomato juice,
I like tomato juice.
I have to have tomato juice."
Announced to the open air,
Then aside to someone at a table,
"Did you know that tomato juice
Comes from red cows?"

Wow! So much for listening! It reminded her of the age old question about a tree crashing in the abandoned forest. With no one to hear it, did it really make a sound? Does the poem belong to the speaker or to the hearer, the assembler? Then just behind and to the side of her she witnessed and heard this scene:

ALARM BELLS

Scooted dangerously down
In the seat of her wheelchair,
She was lifted up,
Scooted to safety by an aide.
Her alarm sounded!
A nearby resident smilingly said,
"She's here with bells on!"

Humor and potential for poetry are everywhere. She had been trying to encourage other residents to write their own stories. At her previous retirement complex she had lead a writer's group with some success, but here she had no takers yet. A local church was sponsoring a writers' club. Perhaps? Or would it be a better route to suggest that a new program be begun by the Activities Department. Maybe the two ideas could work together. She would have to think about it. Hearing, listening to conversations, to music. Poetry is a form of music. Rhythm, sound. Music to the ears. Time! Energy!

She remembered playing "The 1812 Overture" for her children and having her startled almost 2 year old son run up to her when the cannon fire portion began. "Mommy, who are they shooting at?" He asked. Children have a heightened special sense. They know things that adults tend to forget. She remembered the exact timing of the incident because they moved to Aurora the very next day which was the day before his second birthday. Opportunities for drama and creativity are everywhere, even in chaos of moving.

Memory of attending a Shakespearean production in Oklahoma City with three college professors of Literature popped to the surface. They had taken two college roommates, both English majors, to see this lavish production to introduce them to a whole new realm of culture. As the audience exited the theater, two pseudo intellectual socialite women were making snipping , critical remarks.

"His intonation was off. And those costumes were not true period designs." Dr. J--, a bird-like lady, was so incensed, she said in her oration voice for their benefit at daring to spoil a student's enthralled mood, "It must be a shame to be so educated that one never enjoys a thing!" She and her roommate exchanged amused, knowing glances of recognition and stifled a giggle. What a real educational breakthrough moment it was to hear that a revered, tiny teacher was a fighter with a temper to add to her voice. What a welcome shout of support that was from a champion! He that hath ears, let him hear.

ENCHANTED ISLAND

Again and again she drew
The imaginary island
And colored it a shiny, sunny yellow
Surrounded by a royal blue shoreline
Awash in the roaring waves of a blue-green sea.
No one would ever know that she was
Afraid of water and could not swim.
A friend accused that she was not learning
Just to prove he could not teach her,
But she could float there silently
Island-ward any time SHE chose.

Music and poetry are all around everyone even in her own head, if she chose to hear. Listen, really listen, for there is drama, tragedy, laughter, poetry all around us. But just lately some people seemed to speak more softly, more swiftly, even mumbled. Ahem, what could this mean? Ears. He that hath ears.........

Suddenly she remembered hearing her three year old daughter chattering under a blanket stretched over a box at the end of the hallway. When she asked her what she was playing she said, "Animal, Mommy." Peeking beneath the blanket she had asked what kind of animal was red with white and navy polka dot top. Her answer was: "A Cynthia Ann-imal, Mommy...!"

Children have a gift of language that sounds like music! There is need for supportive, dedicated listeners. Where are the listeners? We can re-awaken it, if we try.

She awoke from a dream about caring for her three year old daughter who was suffering from an ear infection, fondling her curls away from her face and singing softly until she fell asleep. She turned sleepily on her own bed to discover pain on her left ear. It was folded strangely and painfully against her pillow. Had it triggered her dream? She smiled at remembering her grandfather's oft repeated remark, "God gave us just one mouth and two ears for a very good reason."

Hand

She held out her hands to see long tapered fingers and long nails painted a metallic pink. She admired them with a smile, not out of vanity, but out of thankfulness. There was no inflamed soreness across the backs or in the joints today. So many residents had gnarled arthritic hands. Her red soreness came and went. Sometimes it was difficult to raise the fork to her mouth. Pain and stiffness made even signing her name difficult and holding a newspaper or a book a task. She wondered at the sight of the hands of other residents and pondered the tasks they had performed in their life times. She looked over at a woman at a nearby breakfast table, studying her hands, for she knew that she arranged the flowers in vases on the dining tables for the activities staff when blossoms were available. The saying "Idle hands are the devil's workshop" which her grandmother often quoted, popped in her mind. This was immediately followed by the remembered voice of her mother observing, "You have the longest nails and the hardest calluses of any kid in the county."

She was taken back to the heat of the cotton patch and the hard handle of a hoe killing weeds left behind when her father cultivated the thick green rows of cotton. Sunflowers, Russian thistles (tumble weeds), goat heads, devil claws, careless weeds and sometimes a patch of Johnson grass remained to infest the field with unwanted plants.

They had to be dug out to leave all the rainfall (if any) to nurture the cotton crop. Blisters and hard, sore calluses built up on her palms and those of her younger brothers as well as those of her parents and grandparents. Involuntarily her hand went up to her sweaty, stiff, salt ladened hair to push it back under the remembered slat bonnet.

She remembered snatches from the book THE WORST HARD TIME, a New York Times best seller, she had just finished reading. She had thought that their southwestern Oklahoma tenant farm had experienced the worst of the dust bowl, but she learned from Egan's documentation that Baca County of Colorado and Dalhart, Texas along with the Oklahoma Panhandle had been hardest hit along the middle of the entire nation. She had written VICTORIOUS, her childhood personal history, so her children and grandchildren would know who they are. They had Oklahoma roots which did not blow away to California and that she was a victorious Oklahoman although her father did not own a square inch of land until she went away to O U graduate school.

Victorious was the meaning of Coffey, her Irish maiden name. She tried always to live up to that name's meaning. She refused to allow anyone to call her an Okie, for that was not who she was. They had stayed home and more than survived. There was no alternative. They were victorious, tenant farming Oklahomans. Then later her new life made a family with four children to provide for and educate.

Hands are for work, for creating, for caressing, for applauding, for quilting, for sewing, for sawing wood, for whittling and for working on the tractor or car motors. They are for searching pages of reference books, for writing research papers and lately for the mysteries of internet information and the joy of creating letters and novels on the computer keyboard.

Her mother said that she was an artist except she worked with fabric not paints. She turned chicken feed sacks into dresses or school shirts and the scraps of material became quilts. Flour sacks became tea towels or kitchen curtains. Hands demanded and delivered many skills. Her quilts still remained a tribute to her loving skills right this moment in the form of a green maple leaf design with a pink border which comforts and warms her granddaughter's husband in his recliner during his lingering illness. They decorate rooms of family and covered her coffin the day of her memorial service as a final tribute from a thoughtful granddaughter. The pattern was called colonial doll.

Smiling, she remembered that first day of teaching the senior class at a small rural high school. She had prepared an exciting presentation for English literature and stood before a class of 10 girls and two boys speaking with enthusiasm. She almost became distracted because the girls watched so intently. Their eyes were riveted on her every movement, every gesture. She kept thinking, "I really worked to make this an interesting lesson, but this level of attention is a little much!"

Toward the end of the class she paused to ask whether any of the students had questions. A girl who was obviously the leader of the class gasped with excitement, "Yes, what color is your nail polish?" Deflated she answered, "Frosted pink cloud by Revlon." End of lesson. Hands command unintended attention sometimes. And yet she could not help swallowing a giggle at herself because of this episode. One never knows who and what she may be teaching or not teaching..

Her portable Smith Corona typewriter came to mind. It was bought with $48. worth of cotton patch sweat.. She had hoed cotton for a neighbor to earn it because she could not imagine learning fast enough to pass typing class without owning her own typewriter. What a treasure! All the way through the rest of high school, college, graduate school it followed her--through papers, news articles and features, scripts for her weekly radio program,

THIS WEEK AT SOUTHWESTERN, poetry, catalog cards for library lab assignments, and a draft manuscript of VICTORIOUS, that keyboard kept her hands busy.

One outstanding memory involving that typewriter and her college roommate stuck with her through many years. Well past midnight the roommate had kept typing on a delayed deadline-pushing paper in the dorm room during finals week. She struggled to sleep with the light on and typewriter clicking away. Several final tests loomed just hours away in the morning. Still the typing went on and on. She called the roommate's name finally and said, "If ever you pull this late night stunt again I will throw you and that typewriter out the window even though it is MY typewriter!"

From across the room came the voice of her roommate, "If I ever postpone doing a paper this long I'll jump out the window all by myself!" They both laughed, for the dorm room was on first floor and all of three feet off the ground. To top it all off, this was their last semester as college seniors. Hands clasp friendships also. It was good that the center had an activities department. Crafts and fund raising projects helped keep idle hands busy. Not everyone is capable of or interested in entertaining himself with reading and writing projects.

Step

One, two, three! Three sets of twenty kicks, three times to experi-ence Physical Therapy and Occupational Therapy. She learned something new each time through. Walkers, electrodes, exercises. Patience and experience, a search for confidence and balance was her conclusion. She was offered an opportunity to be given a motorized chair which she refused, in favor of discipling her body to be as mobile as it was capable of being.

The first time in therapy was triggered by blood clots in the left groin and a massive bleed which left her unable to walk, get out of bed or do much of anything. Staffing of the center as a whole left her wondering what she would ever be able to do. It was difficult to use her hands even to feed herself or write. Finally a single therapist took an interest in her and began coming in early to get her out of bed and initiated a exercise regime. One day the therapist smacked a walker down before her wheelchair and told her to stand. Casually she said, "I wonder whether you can walk." She did walk seven feet.

Then it was 14, 21, 57, 100 and so on until she was able to go to her retirement apartment with temporary 24 hour supervision. Then she was independent of any assistance. She managed to care for herself and wheel herself down to meals and meetings as well as to enjoy her apartment using a lift chair, a shower bench and a standard hospital bed. After several months of independence, a pressure wound appeared on her right ankle and she was hospitalized. The wound (a venous insufficiency ulcer) was vile and developed into a case of MRSA. Again she was so weak that she was unable to walk. Physical and Occupational programs were tried. It was a struggle in spite of concentrated effort on her part and that of the therapists. Medications and the drainage of strength left her performance erratic. Good days were followed by very bad ones. At times her legs felt like wet noodles. Some days she could walk with some success and other days she felt as if the walker would flip up in her face even if she were able to arise from the wheelchair. The parallel bars helped her to walk, but when she got to the end she had to walk backward to the awaiting wheelchair, for she could not make herself let go of the two bars long enough to pivot and return to the wheelchair going forward.

The assigned doctor diagnosed her as suffering from a rare form of arthritis which suddenly appears for no cause and can last for one or two years and disappear just as mysteriously. The center changed off to an air mattress for comfort and to protect against bed sores. The weakness in her muscles aggravated by the movement of the mattress's edge caused spasms in her back which were screamable offenses! Pain made the leg muscles which were strong enough to work refuse to do so. By the end of the prescribed term of the program, not enough progress was documented to justify continued treatment. She was assigned to the long term wing of the center. She was dependent upon staff and lift equipment for all mobility. This caused her to give up her apartment in the independent living complex and agree to long term care at the center. Third time is the charm? After months of being dependent upon the lifts and complete assistance of staff, when census in Re-Hab permitted it, she was approached by a therapist about trying again to gain strength to walk. After performing numerous skills building exercises and application of electronic techniques gradually she was able to stand up readily to the exercise pole, but was not able to pivot and be seated on the raised mat bench. Then came walking along the parallel bars where she was able to pivot, turn and return to the wheelchair. No anxiety. Practice, practice, practices. Numerous strengthening exercises were interspersed beginning at 6 a.m. and lasting until breakfast was served in the dining room. The cooperative work of both Occupational and Physical Therapy programs made the difference, she believed. Transfers from the recliner lift chair to the wheelchair using the walker, then transfers from the wheelchair to the commode were the practiced exercises. Walking along the hall to build strength and mobility--Timing and persistence are key steps to recovery. Now for developing greater balance! In her mind she deliberately retraced her Re-Hab experiences as a source of self examination and reassurance. Progress is on-going. She watched the therapists and their approach to coaxing performance out of patients. One whimpered and said, "I can't. It hurts." The therapist said, "That's exactly why we are working on this. You need to get better." She thought, "That's a good way to deal with her. Acknowledge her feelings, but don't allow that to impede progress." Of course, she was not as charitable in her thoughts when techniques were directed at herself! Eureka! She used the lift chair to aid standing up to the walker and side-stepping, pivoting into the waiting wheelchair. Then she and the therapist headed for the Re-Hab gym for the 6 a.m. session. This became the daily routine. The same skill was applied to getting to the commode when the Occupational Therapist came into her room. Transferring those techniques to CNAs was the next step; then applying the same skills to getting in and out of bed remains, and toileting skills also. Step by step! Gaining balance and building skills are required. Learning and re-learning, practice makes almost perfect, one step at a time.

Lady

Patience was a lady! She gasped at the thought of a long ago relative answering a question she had posed to her Mother about the difference between someone being a lady as opposed to a woman. Patience Paynter Bullock was the wife of William Bullock who was from Bermuda and a sea captain--a Scot or an Englishman. Patience was the mother of Stephen Bullock also a sea captain between Bermuda and Charleston during the late 1600's and early 1700's. Stephen married Marie, a Spanish girl, and they became the parents of Mary who married Rene de St. Julien, a tall red haired French Huguenot soldier. He fled France for religious freedom in Holland and became part of William and Mary's beloved Dutch Guard as King and Queen of England, but eventually came to the new world. All this ran through her mind as she reviewed family history.

Contact with distant cousins gave her stories about Patience, a Quaker, often in difficulty with the Church of England for failure to pay tithes to the church although she was not a member in the first place. She also had stepped up in defense of Thomas, an indentured servant to whom 30 acres of land had been promised as the result of completion of the term of his indentureship. Without a doubt, Patience was a lady! A woman is a female. She may be good; she may be bad or indifferent. Actions speak louder than words. That is what her Mother had taught her. A lady can grow up in the cotton patch or anywhere. It is her choice to be a lady. Actions certainly speak louder than words. She looked from face to face in the dining room and studied them. When in their lives had they decided to be a Lady as opposed to merely a woman. Was she qualified to judge which was which? Did she know any one of them well enough to determine which was which? Would anyone think she was crazy for entertaining such thoughts? Did she even care whether they thought anything one way or another? What about the staff? Which were women and which could qualify to be a lady.

She chuckled and shook her head at remembering being in the dime store with her Grandmother when a old Negro female approached them at the counter. "How much?" she asked holding up a pair of panties. No answer. Her Grandmother ignored her and she, as an obedient child did not speak to a stranger.

"Grandma," she said, "The Negro lady wants to know the price."

"There is no such thing." was her Grandmother's response. She scowled and shook her head, for she did not understand. The black lady had asked a question of the adult present in a sweet soft voice. Why couldn't she be a lady? Does a lady have to be a lady all the time? "Grandma, what happened that made you so deathly afraid of black people?" Would she ever understand? She did not and could not ask that question.

Her Mother was definitely a lady. She was kind to everyone even the uncle who was "afflicted". The sister-in-law was hateful to him and chased him away when she saw him on the street. Mother looked and acted sweet even in the field when nobody could look like the Lady Esther face powder ad. A lady treats everyone with respect. She remembered having a meaningful conversation with a staff member on a current issue when her daughter came into the room. The staff member's tone and demeanor changed and suddenly she did not exist. The daughter became the only one in the room. She remembered thinking, "When did I leave and where did I go? Am I instantly non-existent, a nothing?" It wasn't intentional, but it was automatic. What is wrong with having a three-way conversation?

Awareness is needed. At times there is a tendency to throw a blanket over everyone and treat everyone as if each is mentally impaired, incompetent. Some are not sharp and aware, but that wasn't always the case; respectfulness is demanded. One never knows when she entertains a lady unaware.

Love

He dropped his luggage in the middle of the street and with the expression of pure joy on his face, ran to her. Then his navy uniform clad arms embraced her with a cry of sheer release; he clasped her to him. In two days they would be married in Clovis, New Mexico. When she awoke she sighed in the warmth of long ago memories. All those years ago! University degree on the G I bill and the birth of four children flew through her mind.

Love is wonderful and moves rapidly through years of losses and gains. No one here would really understand, but then they had their own memories of love, loss and family events. She could honor their individual memories by listening to their stories. She longed to get them to write them down for themselves; for once they were gone the stories were gone, too. Perhaps there was a child or grandchild in that family who would love stories enough to write them down or at least tell them to each other in snatches of memories. She must work on that project.

She remembered her mother repeating the report of their elderly baby-sitter when the grandparents had come for a visit. "I just want you to know that I have never seen this refrigerator empty. That isn't so in lots of homes where I care for kids." Times were hard during university days with new babies, rent and other needs, but her husband's and her jobs made provision. He bought groceries, coloring books, parkas and warm boots. The G I bill helped with educational expenses. This reflected things he had not known during his own childhood. His mother did not sew. She did piece work, ironing in a factory. Love means providing some how.

She smiled at the memory of the little booklets her Mother created from white paper sacks from Hart's Five and Dime store. Scissors, folding of pages and a well placed seam along the fold made a book on which Mother drew a bunny, a chicken and a snake (only because it was easy to draw, for she hated snakes beyond description.) Why buy a coloring book when you can make your own for nothing? The first "book" she ever wrote was on such a creation and contained a little collection of poems for Mother's Day. Love is priceless.

She treasured family visits here at the care center. These met needs before they were even recognized by the resident. Respect paid to other residents and their families makes the care center bearable. She encouraged herself by remembering and often repeating a Lincoln quotation to herself: "I reckon a man is as happy as he makes up his mind to be."

"Jesus Loves Me--this I know". A sweet, thin, little, old voice came from a room after church service was over. A wife was singing to her husband. He was calm, serene in the thought. Her frequent visits and gentle ways made him calm usually. There was a distinct difference in his demeanor now than when she was gone. Sometimes he wailed loudly in a voice of ghouls and goblins in a haunted house. Occasional utterance of the word PAIN was the only recognizable word she heard him say for the longest time. Then one day as she went by his wheelchair, she said, "Good Morning." He responded, "Morning." and then she was gone by. He was quiet during church service, but then his wife was with him. Love is very good medicine. Sometimes even her presence was not enough, for he was not always aware of her, for then he went way back to the days when he was in a concentration camp and everyone around then was a Nazi. There were few ways to reach through that horror. Staff tried with a special shave and shower. He was loved. He was a neat person, lost in time.

In the case of another resident and her husband, she observed them walking arm in arm or hand in hand which made her content. She met them in the hallway and spoke, calling them each by name. He responded with a cheerful voice. Her expression was flat, unknowing; making no sound of recognition. She could not help wondering whether the wife even knew who held her arm so lovingly. At that moment she was in nowhere world. She had spoken with her a few months before about embroidering bird quilt blocks with such pride. Did that person still exist or was she on vacation permanently? She wondered and even feared to think of that. His attentiveness and faithfulness to visit daily impressed her as a great example of years of love given. He must be living on memories of love shared long ago, memories of when sons were young.. Love is giving and not necessarily receiving in kind. She could not escape the thought of admiration of President Ronald Reagan in his open announcement that he had Alzheimer's. His last great loving gift to the American people, letting them know what fate awaited him in the future which he faced openly, bravely, was shown in this announcement.

Each breakfast time a male resident sought out ladies who had not yet been served coffee by staff members. He addressed them as "Dear" and offered tomato juice, too. He even moved chairs to a more useful spot along the table sides. He needed some way to expend his energy and chose service as a means of doing it. Service is a form of love.

She remembered when her four brothers sneaked away from her to go skinny dipping down on the creek, leaving her to play alone. They came back blistered from head to toe, especially the youngest and fairest of the boys. He was absolutely cooked and could not stand to put on underclothes or to lie under a sheet, but he did not whimper or cry. He said years later how he remembered that she had chopped cotton to buy Noxzema for her complexion and slathered it on his very sore six year old blistered bottom. He said he had never felt anything so cool and comforting in his whole life and how he appreciated such a loving gift that he hadn't even had to ask for. Love is little things forgotten by one, but long remembered by another.

Love is also the sharing of quiet reading time, an ice cream cone surprise, a bit of news from recently received letter or e-mail. Love is happiness. Happiness is a decision. Happiness is contagious. Spread it around. Smile. Love is worship. That thought prompted her to reach for her writing entitled 'RADIATE HIS GLORY', a collection of devotional poems, narratives and scriptures which she began to edit anew for small typo errors. God is Love the Bible says.

Radiate His Glory

In the beginning God created the heaven and the earth.
And the earth was without form and void; and darkness
was upon the face of the deep. And the Spirit of God moved
upon the face of the waters. And God said, "Let there be light!"
And there was light. Genesis 1:1-3

In a Bible study taught by a visiting scholar and pastor of a neigh-
boring church, I learned many things; the messenger and his
scholarly sources dealing with the Hebrew and the Greek I have
forgotten, but I pray that I shall never forget the message he deliv-
ered to me and others when I was much in need of it.

The Hebrew word for light used in the scripture above is the
word for all light, not just sunlight as would automatically come
to mind. Sunlight was not specifically created until verses 14 - 18.
The word used concerning the lights in the firmament actually
means "light holders". That in itself is intriguing, but an astound-
ing truth becomes clear when one realizes that when Jesus said, "I
am the Light of the world" the word used there means ALL LIGHT.
(John 8- 12)

And now are you ready for this? When the Lord said in His Sermon on the Mount, "Ye are the light of the world." (Matthew 5:14) the word used there is light holder. Jesus declared, "I am all the Light there is in this world. Those of you who belong to me are light holders. It is My Light, but because you are mine I make you a light holder."

Ye are the light of the world. A city that is set on a hill cannot be hid. .Neither do men light a candle and put it under a bushel, but on a candlestick; and it giveth light unto all that are in the house. Let your light so shine before men that they may see your good works, and glorify your Father which is in heaven. (Matthew 5:14-16)

This portion of his teaching was so compelling that I searched the scriptures for portions on light. First I discovered several relating to the Baby Jesus and pondered about the bright light which announced His birth. Even the prophecies of Isaiah use the symbol of light to foretell the coming of the Christ Child. (Isaiah 60:1-2)

Arise, shine; for thy Light is come and the glory of the Lord is risen upon thee. For behold, the darkness shall cover the earth, and gross darkness the people: but the Lord shall arise upon thee, and His glory shall be seen upon thee. Moreover, the light of the moon shall be as the light of the sun, and the light of the sun shall be sevenfold, as the light of seven days, in the Lord bindeth up the breach of His people and healeth the stroke of their wound. (Isaiah 6:36)

Holy, Holy, Holy, is the Lord of hosts: the whole earth is full of His glory. (Isaiah 6:3b)

After studying and pondering the scriptures above I could not escape the thought that the moon is a dead and dark planet. It has no light of its own. All moonlight we see is actually reflected light from the sun. But Genesis 1:16 declares the lesser light, the moon, to be a light holder.

We as Christians have no light of our own. Any light we have to give is His light. We are but the vessel, the light holder. I began to consider the relationship of the sun and the moon and as I did the poem below gradually took shape in my heart. I share it with you.

RADIATE HIS GLORY

No light have I, Lord
Apart from Thy Son,
Dark as the moon is dark,
Apart from the sun.

Lord, I would seek
A translucence of soul.
To dark hidden corners
I would not hold.

May Thy laser light
Penetrate to the far depths of me.
And may the light that shines out
Be the image of Thee!

Carrying the symbols a step farther, I began to think about the lunar eclipse and how I must appear to those persons watching my Christian example. Imagine using a large yellow circle of construction paper to represent Christ. A small circle of the same paper is almost invisible against the larger one. Imagine, for the sake of Biblical symbolism, the world as a black circle. The closer you are to an individual and the closer the black circle is between their eye and you the less of Christ in you can be seen. What is closer to you than Jesus? Whatever is closer is blocking their view of you and therefore is the bushel so to speak under which your candle is hidden, the world which eclipses the sun. Without the sun, the moon has no light to give. I must state the obvious for the sake of emphasis. Without Christ in me I have no light at all.

Vision without light is impossible. Both beauty and danger are hidden in darkness. Since "the Light of the world is Jesus" as the old hymn declares, those who are outside Him remain in spiritual darkness. What of those who accept Him as Savior and then gradually close their eyes and minds to His illumination and stubbornly refuse to grow? What of those who say they know Him and yet every beam which would give evidence of His presence and glory in their life is filtered through an earthbound smog?

Conviction of my own heart prompts this pursuit. All Christians have felt the convicting guilt with which Paul struggled in recognition of the frailty of man in controlling his own will and destiny. A tired sigh of, "Why fight it?" typifies how little we really try to grow in closeness and likeness to Christ We too readily surrender to the everyday tedium of the world's pressures and demands, ignoring the beauty available to each of us in Christ.

These words of Ralph Waldo Emerson apply, "Though we travel the world over to find the beautiful, we must carry it with us or we find it not." As Paul said in his letter to the Colossians in chapter 1 verse 27, "Christ in you, the hope of Glory!" What is the main characteristic of a Christian? (Originally the term Christian was "Christ one". It was a term of derision, a put down.) We have taken that name so lightly and have used it in so broad a context that it would seem that "Christ one" might be a preferable term for those Christians who sincerely mean business. It indicates more forcefully one who belongs to and is a follower of Christ. It is His beauty, His light, His strength that lives in the "Christ one". Allowing Him to live in us is the only hope of finding any beauty or light; even the strength or ability to carry light or beauty is God-given.

As we have indicated previously, the moon is a dead body, lifeless. It has no illumination of its own. Its source of light is sunlight reflected back earthward. The Christian is as the moon and the sun, the Son of God. A space probe and a voice from space saying to all the world, "In the beginning God..." should have stirred the heart of every Christian, but there are also deeper, hidden truths to be gleaned from this sun-moon study. The Christian is faced with the challenge given by the Master in the Sermon on the Mount, "Ye are the light of the world." (Matthew 5:14.) It is not, however, until the Christian sees himself literally as the moon, void and dark, in our own strength, that he can begin to realize the complete implication of Christ Jesus' words, "Ye are the light of the world." Recognizing Christ in the truth of his declaration, "I am the Light of the world: he that followeth Me shall not walk in darkness, but shall have the light of life." (John 8:12) is the first step toward Christian growth, toward spiritual enlightenment, toward spiritual empowerment. This view of our intended, close and harmonious relationship with Christ is phenomenal when we actually see Him as He is:

JESUS, LORD

Jesus is perfect love
In a world of snarling hate.
Jesus is perfect sanity
In a world gone mad.

Jesus is perfect sacrifice
In a world grabbing not giving.
Jesus is perfect joy
In a world a-quake with cries.

Jesus is perfect order
In a world chaotic.
Jesus is perfect wisdom
In a world of senseless knowledge.

Jesus is perfect light
In a world of satanic darkness.

> Jesus is perfect bread
> In a world of gnawing hunger.
> Jesus is perfect peace
> In a world of constant war.
>
> Jesus is perfection;
> In His will is my only peace,
> My only bread, light, wisdom,
> Only order, joy and sacrifice,
> Only sanity and love.
> JESUS, ----LORD!

One spiritual experience involving light stays most vividly in my mind. Awe, humility, excitement and a more than healthy case of stage fright encompassed our small church choir as we marched upon the risers. The concert for the Ministers of Music of the national convention was in a larger church and this strangeness added to our fear. The early hour gave us little warm-up time. From the beginning the words of encouragement and admonition from our Minister of Music were, "Worship! That is the only reason for this concert. Unless we worship, they can not worship with us. Do not expect applause. We can not possibly compare with their own big choirs in any way except quality of worship. If we concentrate on worshipping the Lord, then the music will take care of itself."

Classic hymns, spirituals, and contemporary numbers were in the program. I had wondered why he had selected Bach's "Break Forth Oh Beauteous Heavenly Light" to begin. "Why not the spiritual," I thought. " Now that would wake them up!" God's perfect plan knew something none of us had counted on during that early morning concert. Only a tinge of nervousness colored those first words, "Break forth! Oh, beauteous heavenly Light and usher in the morning!" We were suddenly overwhelmingly aware of light pouring in the top half of the stained glass windows like so many spotlights bathing the bright red carpet in sunlight. Until just that crucial moment, the sunlight had been blocked by the lodge hall directly east across the street. The joy of affirmation released us to profound worship. It was not our long hours of practice nor even the unquestionable skill of our director to pull music from our predominately untrained voices, but God's own timing and plan. Coincidence? Really?

We were not performers, but worshippers, instruments for God's action. We were merely "light holders" testifying to His Glory. When the Ministers of Music not only applauded, but stood to applaud, we all knew that we had shared the worship of the Lord. God's Light showed us His presence in a vividly visible way. His spiritual Light brightens sometimes more subtly progressive as we grow, read the Bible and seek to know Him.

...And they need no candle, neither light of the sun; for the Lord God giveth them light: and they shall reign for ever and ever. Revelation 22:5

I, Jesus have sent mine angel to testify unto you these things in the churches. I am the root and offspring of David, and the bright and morning star. Revelation 22: 16

And the city had no need of the sun, neither of the moon to shine in it: for the glory of God did lighten it, and the Lamb is the light thereof.. Revelation 21: 23

The Light of the world is Jesus.

Believing Is Seeing

A two by two inch square of plastic was given me by a salesman who called on our library. On it, in the form of micro images the whole Bible was printed. The thought and technology involved in making that possible is enough to stagger the mind. It takes a reader with a powerful lens to read that ultra microfiche and, of course, it takes a light source to make those images seeable--readable to the human eye. It is possible by using a reader/ printer to print-out any chapter or verse chosen from the Bible, to capture it on paper. That thought was intriguing enough to occupy my mind for a while and then, of course, another idea captured my imagination, for there is a big difference in depth of understanding between seeing and reading--between reading and comprehending and on and on.

Then the Lord called to my memory Luke 1:46 where Mary after being told by the angel that Jesus would be born to her, began a song of praise, "My soul doth magnify the Lord!" My first thought was "Mary that is the strangest thing I ever heard of! It is impossible to make God bigger than He already is! I have a hard time bringing into focus what I already know of Him without making Him bigger--Ah, ho! In magnifying something, the object of magnification is not changed--it is a whole new way of seeing! My ability to see is changed! God is the same yesterday, today and forever --unchanging from everlasting to everlasting--forever and ever. Amen! In order to magnify the Lord I must accept His power in me. I must allow His Holy Spirit to reveal Himself in a new light with a new lens which makes Him, the Invisible and Ever-present God visible enough that I can say vividly, sincerely something my daughter once said to me at age 4:

> Mommy,
> Did you know---
> Prayer is like
> Kissing God?

> And you say
> The prayer
> 'Cause you can't really
> Hug His neck?

When she said that to me I suddenly knew anew what the scripture means "of such is the kingdom of heaven." Out of the mouths of babes!

The world of science says, "Seeing is believing," but God says, "Believing is seeing!" As your faith is, so be it unto you. "Faith is the SUBSTANCE of things hoped for the EVIDENCE of things not seen." according to Hebrews 11: 1 . In God's realm, "Believing truly is seeing." Knowing this, along with the psalmist I extend the invitation:

"O magnify the Lord with me, and let us exalt His Name io-gether!" Psalm 34:3

Slowly as I gave more and more thought to these ideas, a poem took form in my heart to enable me to "preach" to myself and learn more truths which the scripture had for me.

SPIRITUAL SIGHT

Be not mini-minded, oh, my soul,
Seeing only with carnal eyes.
If I truly know Him I shall
Grow in spiritual perception.
The infant Christian perceives a little
And even those who seek the perfection which
Paul sought, "see as through a glass darkly."

Why, then do I limit God by stunting
That capacity to grow which He gives?
Why, when submission to God,
Seeking knowledge of Him,
Is the most mind and soul expanding
Experience available to man?
Be not mini-minded, oh, my soul!

And be not conformed to this world; but be ye transformed by the renewing of your mind, that ye may prove what is that good and acceptable, and perfect, will of God. Romans 12: 3

Conformed or transformed? That is indeed a burning question. The background meaning of the word "hypocrite" is "play-actor," a pretender. Even when one professes to belong to Jesus, it is easy to fall into the trap of image-maker, pretending to be something on the outside when we are something very different on the inside. Surface, cosmetic Christianity invades the organized church at times, but as an old country preacher once said in my hearing, "When you let the hypocrite in the church stand between you and God, just remember that he is closer to God than you are." Now to examine the pretense in our lives:. Each of us want to be well-thought-of. We wish to be seen as a good, faithful, loyal Christian. Comparisons of the way I wish to be seen, the way I see myself and the way God sees me, the way I really am, caused me to write this "light-hearted" (?) poem which I subtitled "Coppertone Christian".

CHILD OF LIGHT

The sense of a sunflower,
Lord, give to me,
Face turned upward
To seek light of Thee.

I must not bear
A counterfeit devotion.
Mere pretense of Presence
Is just suntan lotion.

"For ye were sometimes darkness, but now are ye light in the Lord. Walk as children of light." Ephesians 5: 8

One day when I was seated in my office during the noon hour puzzling over the selection of the best candidate for a position, I reached for a glass prism. As it sat on the corner of my desk the sun shone on and through it making a "rainbow" of light on the wall. I noticed how the rainbow pattern was broken by the name of the firm whose advertising it bore. I could not help applying that symbol to the ego of a Christian. I kept thinking of the old almost trite saying, "What you are speaks so loud, I can't hear what you say."

Suddenly I tied these thoughts to my lifelong fascination with the joy of the rainbow. Since I grew up in dust bowl days, rainbows and rain were special gifts of God to me. To Noah and his family the rainbow was God's promise that never again would God destroy the earth by flood, but somehow to me the gift of rain and the rainbow to top it off were special symbols of God's generosity and blessing. Somehow my thoughts returned to the Lord's declaration, "I am the Light of the world." The rainbow breaks down the various colors of light in all its beauty for us to see. The prism I held in my hand and the black images printed on its surface made me think once again that ego and self of a Christian have to take on translucence for God's brilliance to show through. The red rose absorbs all other colors and radiates only the color red. That is why we see it as red. The singleness of purpose is the ideal toward which the Christian strives.

"Behold, what manner of love the Father hath bestowed upon us, that we should be called the sons of God: therefore the world knoweth us not because it knew Him not. Beloved, now are we the sons of God, and it doth not yet appear what we shall be: but we know that when He shall appear we shall be like Him: for we shall see Him as He is. I John 3: 1-2.

He that saith he is in the light, and hateth his brother, is in darkness even until now. He that loveth his brother abideth in the light, and there is none occasion of stumbling in him. But he that hateth his brother is in darkness, and walketh in darkness, and knoweth not whither he goeth, because that darkness hath blinded his eyes. I John 2: 9-11.

In Weakness We Are Made Strong

Quietly, humbly he came into the meeting room, this newly elected student body president from an African nation. He had asked permission to speak at our college Baptist Student Union meeting. With more than a little curiosity we waited. We wondered and speculated about what he might say. The campus rumor-mill said that he had been nominated for president in the first place because campus political climate was not then ready for an American black to be elected and a dozen or so variations on that theme. It was a time of unrest and harsh feelings among many groups and individuals on campus.

We were totally unprepared for what we heard after opening prayer and the introduction of our guest. "In my country," he said, "The only Americans I have ever known were missionaries, kindly, Christian people. My picture of the United States was one of heaven on earth where all people were Christian, concerned and above all honest and loving. Sad to say it simply is not so." He paused and looked around the room one by one at the handful of members present. "I recognize in this group a very strong CHRIST-

FORCE. I have come to ask your prayers, for without them during this year in office I simply will not make it!" After prayer for God's blessing upon each of us for the year ahead, our guest left quietly and humbly, just as he had come.

We were very different. "I recognize in this group a very strong CHRIST-FORCE..." Those words bounced around the room, echoed in our ears, minds and more importantly pierced the hearts of each of us. At the time of that meeting the Baptist Student Union which I sponsored was a very small group. We were a little disheartened. The campus was plagued with rumbles and grumbles about war and rumors of war, about racial tensions and questioning of everything valued. We were discouraged, small and weak, but in the mind of a stranger, a foreigner, we were a CHRIST-FORCE. We sat there for quite some time silent, stunned.

Finally when we were able to speak, someone said, "He came to us for help, but he helped us more than he knows."

"CHRIST-FORCE! I am so glad that English isn't his native language, for I am sure he would not have used those two words together, if---"

"We don't really have any power and very little influence on campus, but Christ does have. We've been acting as if we had to do everything for ourselves, by ourselves, and Oh, WOW!"

On and on spontaneous disconnected phrases flowed at odd intervals. Tears brimmed. I did not trust myself to say very much because my heart was so full. It was better that each person deal with the words of our guest in his own way. Prayer and special attentive support through our BSU president plus occasional quick visits to my Library office by the student body president constituted the contact. It was a different group which I sponsored from then on. One vivid example I cite as evidence of the difference. The BSU president, basically a very shy person, was called to the ministry and eventually became a foreign missionary. Even now, years later, when I hear news of that African nation, the devastating drought and famine there, I remember that former student body president and pray that awareness of the true CHRIST-FORCE is still with him.

DYNAMO WITHIN

Part I
Who can stand in these days
When peace and patriotism are words suspect?
Helplessness, apathy, hopelessness abound.
How weak I am in my own strength
To stem the tide
To shape the acts of men.
But I do stand, reach out, declare,
For I have a DYNAMO within.
Jesus said, "Be not afraid, go tell brethren....All power is given
unto Me in heaven and earth Matthew 28:10b--18b
Therefore I take pleasure in infirmities, in reproaches, in necessi-
ties, in persecutions, in distresses for Christ's sake: for when I am
weak, then am I strong. II Corinthians 12:10

Part II
Ego-centric man, ---self centered,
Is a very small circle with a vacuum in the middle!
He tries desperately to fill the void
With I, ME, MY,
But emptiness remains there
Unsatisfied, insatiable!

Christo-centric man recognizes
That he is nothing, but with the indwelling Christ
Vacuum is truly filled.
CHRISTO-CENTRICITY, Christ-centeredness is
Life's power and meaning.
He is the DYNAMO within.

Without ME ye can do nothing. John 15:5c

Part III
The Christian life is three concentric circles.
I am in Christ and He is in me.
The Christ-life practices Christo-centricity
The ego circle becomes less and less conspicuous
As the DYNAMO grows within.

And to know the love of Christ, which passeth knowledge, that ye might be filled with all the fullness of God. Ephesians 3:19

With all boldness ...Christ shall be magnified in my body, whether it be by life or by death. For me to live is Christ. Philippians 1:20-21

The Greek word translated as power in English is the root word for dynamo. We have a powerful God who spoke this universe into existence and who is willing to empower us to do great things, but Whom we limit in our lives because of fear, laziness, blindness at times. Look back at the chapter BELIEVING IS SEEING and the poem "Spiritual Sight."

How do we serve God anyway? Is prayer and piety all there is to it? Years ago I had a pastor who told his church, "You can't give God a loaf of bread." He was saying in the name of Jesus we can give man a loaf of bread, but God expects of us service to our fellow man to His glory and honor. This pastor came to the above conviction, because of a series of circum-stances built around false accusations he was put in jail. A hot-shot district attorney was almost able to make it his perma-nent home for a number of years. This experience taught the pastor compassion he had never known before. He established a prison ministry. It taught that small college town church family that God intends that we support and encourage one another even if it means mortgaging our home as one church member did to make bail for our pastor. As a wide-eyed, law-abiding, law- revering college student, I learned and remembered that "Caring Costs."

CARING COSTS

Caring costs.
How much am I willing to pay?
The Master paid more than I can fathom
To purchase His redeemed ones.
Not for redemption, but because of it,
What service shall I give?
Caring costs;
Reach out to others in concern,
In love, in warning!
Caring costs--energy, time, self.
Caring costs. It also pays.

By love serve one another. For all law is fulfilled in one word, even this; Thou shalt love thy neighbor as thyself. Galatians 5: 13c-14

When saw we Thee a stranger, and took Thee in? Or naked, clothed Thee? Or when saw we Thee sick or in prison, came unto Thee? And the King shall say unto them, "Verily, I say unto you, in as much as ye have done it unto the least of these my brethren, ye have done it unto Me." Matthew 25:38-40

In 1983 I was in an accident which could have been catastrophic. It was during rush hour traffic and involved a semi-truck pulling heavy equipment which hit my daughter's small car in which the two of us were passengers. We were hit twice by the semi-truck which caused us to bounce off the concrete median strip twice. Miraculously we hit no other cars and no other cars hit us! I sustained a severely broken ankle. My daughter was badly bruised and her car was totaled. Eventually, although I hung on for over two years, I had to take early medical disability retirement from my faculty position as an academic librarian. On the face of it this was a horrendous blow which caused me to have to retire at least 10 years earlier than I would have. God knows things we could not possibly know and would be frantic if we did know ahead of time. That weakness, that disability caused me to retire and stay home. It gave me two years at home with my husband that I would not have had. What I did not know was that my husband would die September 3, 1987.

In the insurance trial the opposing counsel had been especially harsh and arrogant even knowing that he was in the hospital and gravely ill. It was almost at the end of the trial he had died, but as they say "The show must go on." For the last day of the trial knowing that my husband had just died, opposing counsel brought his wife (a law student) and his entire staff into the court room to sit and face my daughter and me to observe our every move, our every expression wanting an excuse for a mistrial. Our attorney had asked, " Are you sure you can do this?"

I said, "We have to, don't we?" He said, "Well, yes." Then my daughter and I agreed that the only way we could do it was just not to look at each other. When closing arguments were over and the case was turned over to the jury, the wife of the opposing counsel approached us in the hallway of the City and County building to say, "I really have to hand it to you. I didn't think you could do it!"

My daughter said, "That's all right. Our trial is over. You have to take yours home with you."

Even in our weakest times, maybe even because of our weakest times, God provides the foreknowledge, the loving kindness we could not possibly understand, but we can trust Him to give us strength when the time comes. In weakness we are truly made strong.

Stress/Trust Quotient

Professional "junk" mail, ads received at home, news features, radio and television commercials, from every angle managing stress, overcoming stressful situations, this subject is thrown repeatedly before our eyes. Is there a Christian way to deal with stress?

One of the most popular terms applied to stress a few years ago was "uptight," in other terms keyed-up, overwrought, high strung, super-sensitive and on and on. It is preferable to have some feelings than to be so "laid back" or "mellow" that nothing matters at all. When someone says "I couldn't care less" that may, in fact, be true, then again it may only be repressed anger over an event or situation too close to the heart to be talked about safely.

As the saying goes, we are often our own worst enemies, for repressed anger eats away like a canker sore or builds to an explosive state. Anger readily expressed makes enemies. Soon one may become viewed as being so short tempered that getting feelings out in the open too frequently becomes the same as crying "wolf!" until everyone refuses to hear what is being said. Only noise is heard, annoying noise! What does one do then in dealing with hurts and injustices, real or imagined? Pray and search the scriptures, of course. First of all, I must confess to having had to deal with all sorts of feelings in the stress and anger categories during my lifetime--in personal and professional realms. Basically, I am viewed by most of my colleagues and acquaintances as calm and even- tempered sort. Because much of my professional career has involved high levels of people contact, people with problems and frustrations of their own, I have learned to deal with those tensions readily, even with some expertise, if I may be so immodest as to say so. Reality sets in when personal affronts come from "people who should know better."

My Daddy would label them educated fools. Situations which attack my personal integrity have always been very difficult, for my sense of right and wrong is not always identical with those who have authority or political clout. At one particular point in my professional career, the temptation to hate was extreme. A young staff member came to me asking how I could stand a particular high level individual and the situation in general. I had struggled with my feelings and had been unable to resolve anything face-to-face with the offender, but suddenly I knew what to say to this staff person who valued me and would have agreed heartily had I launched a verbal barrage against individuals and injustices in several quarters.

Finally I could say aloud what I had been trying to tell myself, "Hey, I don't know anyone worthy of the energy it would take to hate her or him properly. Why do something if you don't intend to do it right?" The look of astonishment and agreement was rewarding. He even gave a short little laugh when he said, "I never would have thought of it quite that way." I could also tell myself another very important thing: "There are those who had lost something more valuable in that situation than anything I ever intend to lose, that is my respect, personal and professional. "I thank you, Lord, for bringing me through this stressful valley with my personal integrity and self-respect intact."

It was not with a feeling of self-righteousness that I could say that, for I had ignored a lesson God had taught me years before. He had even given me a poem at that time to illustrate it. I must confess to being both a slow learner and a forgetful one, for this is what I learned once and forgot.

UPTIGHT OR UPRIGHT

When tempest and tirade tear at my soul--
Uptight or upright
Christ is the difference.

When flesh and the devil vie for control--
Uptight or upright?
Christ is the difference.

Glorious paradox!
Crucified with Christ
Is to live as one victorious;
And surrendered
Is to stand triumphant!

Uptight or upright
CHRIST makes all the difference.

I applied my heart to know, and to search, and to seek out wisdom, the reason of things, and to know the wickedness of folly, even of foolishness and madness. Lo, this only have I found, that God hath made man upright, but they have sought out many inventions. Ecclesiastes 7:25, 29

Mark the perfect man, and behold the upright, for the end of that man is peace. .Psalm 37:37

Thou will. keep him in perfect peace, whose mind is stayed on Thee because he trusteth in Thee. Isaiah 26:3

There are those who look back to the "good old days" and moan endlessly about how tough things are today. Dealing with the here and now is difficult, for it involves making choices we CAN do something about and for which responsibility will weigh heavily upon us. I am one who grew up in a rural area, so I can relate readily to the pastoral scene of the Twenty Third Psalm or Jesus as the Good Shepherd. My working on a commuter campus with urban students (who earned their mascot's name, "Roadrunners" for good reason) caused me to examine how they might relate to the Twenty Third Psalm and the pastoral setting. (Actually God does not need me to defend His Word or to apologize for its content, but some thought of making His message plain to an audience helps give that message even greater depth to my own heart.) A few years ago on this same urban campus scattered in rental buildings in 23 different street addresses, I had opportunity to plan a building which would be rented back to the college as the Library. It would have windows, floor to ceiling where previous quarters had exceedingly few windows of any size.

I asked whether it might be possible to build a window into my office and the planners agreed to try. What I did not know was that it was very difficult task to accomplish, given the type of building and the location of my future office. When the interior walls began to be erected and I looked out of that longed-for window, I had to laugh uproariously, for the view from my window was the boarded up window in the brick wall of a garage not 10 feet away and a tiny misshapen tree growing stubbornly at the foundation of that wall. That experience tied together with being faculty sponsor of the Baptist Student Union group lead me to write:

A NOW PSALM

Though paths where Thou doest lead me
Be paved with concrete
And the streets are never still,

Thy voice would I hear,
For Thou art ever the Transmitter of Truth.
Lord, make me a proper receiver
Plugged in, turned on, and tuned in to Thee.
"He who hath an ear let him hear," Thou hath said.
Willing ears, give me, Lord, open ears give me!

The cries of the lost are pretense at laughter.
But the loneliness in their eyes and in their silences
Shrieks and sobs in a voicelessness which tears my heart,
Strengthen, Lord, lest I faint,
Or worse still lest I close eyes and ears
To all those lost and crying around me.

Make my neighbor real, oh, Lord.
Help me to know words by Thy definition,
For nihilism or meaninglessness has no place with Thee,
Make my heart Thy dwelling place, for I desire to dwell with
Thee.
The paths of righteousness are nowhere
Unless Christ dwells within.

Fear thou not, for I am with thee; be not dismayed; for I am thy God, I will strengthen thee, yea, I will help thee, yea, I will uphold thee with the right hand of my righteousness. Isaiah 41:10

A few years ago I was experiencing a particularly difficult time, so when I had an appointment with our family doctor he sensed it. He asked what was troubling me in addition to the medical problem. I gave him the essence of the troublesome events I was struggling through at work. I said something about, "It's hard to be constructive and pleasant under those circumstances."

"Always remember, you are a survivor!" he said.

Suddenly I gasped to myself, "No, not just a survivor! I am VICTORIOUS!" You see, victorious is the meaning of my Irish maiden name. Names mean something to God. He changed the names of several Biblical saints when he called him to service and there will come a day when each child of God will. have a new name according to the book of Revelation:

He that hath an ear, let him hear what the Spirit saith unto the churches: To him that overcometh will I give to eat of the hidden manna, and will give him a white stone, and in the stone a new name is written, which no man knoweth saving that receiveth it. Revelation 2:17

Each of us needs to remember who we are and who is our Father. In this strange day and time so many people are tempted to live beyond and above our means. In our relationship with God, however, too often we live far below our station. We deny the support the Father has ready and waiting for us.

During a Bible study on the campus where I worked, a young man shook his head unbelievingly, "I can't believe how dumb I really am sometimes! I am always turning my BLESSINGS into BURDENS! I say, 'Look at all this stuff I have to study. I have two big tests on Monday and it isn't even mid-term yet. They gave me the whole weekend to stew about those tests' and on and on I go complaining and muttering. All that grumbling when actually I am so fortunate to be in school at all! At least I was able to raise enough money for my tuition this term!'" He was a student. That was his role, his calling for that semester, his name, so to speak. He was creating his own stress, his own burdens.

Stress or burdens are not the exclusive property of adults. I became overwhelmingly aware of that more times than one. Children experience total stress, for they can not tell themselves "tomorrow things will be better; I'll work my way out of these problems." One morning I was asked to take charge of the three year olds in Sunday School.

Parents dropped a little boy by the room and left to go to their own classes. The minute the door closed between them he began to cry, yowl and carry on as if his heart would break. No amount of trying to comfort him, divert his attention or any of a dozen tricks I had played to quiet my own children would work on him. He howled long and loud. As he did 13 or 14 children became more upset by his unhappiness. I could not think of how to handle this at first, then I picked up a piece of modeling clay and put it on the corner of the table nearest him. I hit the clay with my knuckles and then with my palm. "You are the noisiest clay I ever heard!" I said, "Why can't you be nice?"

He immediately pushed my hand away from the clay and began to pound on it with all his might. "Naughty, naughty!" he said. "Loud! Shhh!" Then he became silent and less violent in his working with the clay. The quiet that followed allowed me to begin singing a soft, little song and present the short lesson I had prepared for the group. How like that little boy we often are as Christians, for we storm and fret over being left out or not getting our way. This is in contrast to our Biblical admonition from the Sermon on the Mount.

Be ye therefore perfect, even as your Father which is in heaven is perfect. Matthew 5:48

The verse is quite meaningful when read on face value, but too often we become trapped by the literal interpretation of the word perfect without taking into account the actual meaning of the word perfect is mature, grown-up, Christ-like. Could it be that the Lord is sweetly admonishing each of us, "Don't be such a big baby; God isn't. He gives everything." That makes the Christmas scriptures all the more meaningful, for Christ came to earth as an infant and knows what it is to be human.

For we have not a high priest which cannot be touched with the feeling of our infirmities; but was in all points tempted like as we are, yet without sin. Let us therefore come boldly unto the throne of grace that we may obtain mercy, and find grace to help in time of need. Hebrews 4: 15-16

The Lord Jesus is really saying to us in all earnestness and understanding, "I know the temptation of wanting to feel like a cry-baby;

I've been there. But strive to grow up to be all you can be in Me, and I'll be right there helping you each step of the way," Empathy is the strongest means of being an example before non-Christians and Christians, too. Critical attitude or self-righteousness are two pitfalls to guard against, for both the weak Christian and the non-Christian feel a natural urge to pick our Christian example apart. That makes it easier for them to say, "See, I'm not so bad. She has flaws as big as mine!" Being an example is a strange bundle to balance, walking along the tightrope of modern life. Viewers may often be afflicted with astigmatism of their own life's experience. The humps and bumps on the surface of our eyes shape their viewpoints.

A young man with a Hispanic surname was classmate in a course I audited to give me some historical perspective for writing my child's personal history of the dust bowl in Oklahoma. He was also student body president that year. The following semester I saw him in the Library and spoke to him. "Hey, how are things going this term?"

"Oh, I got myself in a bind, for I have enrolled in too many courses in order to finish up." Now that is a legitimate concern, but then he ruined it by saying: "It's pretty tough when you've been dragged back and forth from Colorado to California working the crops when you should have been in school." He said it with just a little too much of an invitation for pity. "Aw, pooh" I blurted out calling him by name. "At least you got to travel, I was stuck in the same cotton patch!"

Both his eyes and his mouth flew open wide; then he gasped, "You pulled cotton!"

"You think you are unique? Was I BORN a faculty member?" I responded. He turned on his heel, but as he turned his face away I observed that he was grinning broadly.

"I knew I wouldn't get an inch off you!" He said softly with amusement.

My point in telling this story is to say that being a Christian example entails loving people enough and SHOWING it, even risking the possibility of offending slightly. Had I sympathized and said something like "Oh, you poor kid!" Or had I mentioned the possibility of racial or cultural disadvantage rather than straightforward identification with him, I would have lost him. He would have gone away feeling sorry for himself for no telling how long. There is such a thing as a sweet and gentle kick in the pants. I know, for the Lord has had to do that for me more times than I care to remember or reveal. He also has sent messengers to tell me similar things which I could later identify as being used by Him to teach me a lesson I desperately needed to know.

Call me a little wacky, but I even believe that God can use inanimate objects to teach us. My computer has "eaten" this chapter or portions of it three times. Why this chapter on stress and not the rest? You tell me. It is a better chapter for the writing and rewriting.

Stress under control can be used by God to teach us many things. A little pressure applied in the right place at the right time is often necessary to get us to move or at least to move in the right direction. When I was a youngster there was a popular song that went like this, "It's what you do with what you got and never mind what you ain't got; it's what you do with what you got that gets there in the end!" The Apostle Paul experienced the stress of a physical problem he asked the Lord to remove. It is good that it is not specifically identified. Each of us have problems from time to time with which Paul's "thorn in the flesh" can help us to deal. This can enrich us spiritually.

"For this thing I have besought the Lord thrice, that it depart from me. And He said unto me, 'My grace is sufficient for thee, for my strength is made perfect in weakness.' Most gladly therefore will I glory in my infirmities, that the power of Christ may rest upon me." II Corinthians 12: 8-9

There is an old saying or proverb: "All sunshine makes a desert." Stress must be balanced with trust in the Lord, for the most worthy Example, offering strength and His own experience in human life that He may provide perfect support for us. We need the hard times to appreciate His help and loving kindness.

Who in the days of His flesh when he had offered up prayers and supplications with strong crying and tears unto Him that was able to save Him from death, was heard in that He feared: Though He were a Son, yet He learned obedience by the things which He suffered; And being made perfect, He became the Author of eternal salvation unto all them that obey Him. Hebrews 5:7-9

For when the time ye ought to be teachers, ye have need that one teach you again the first principles of the oracles of God; and are become such as have need of milk, and not of strong meat. For everyone that useth milk is unskillful in the word of righteousness: for he is a babe. But strong meat belongeth to them that are of full age, even those who by reason of use have their senses exercised to discern both good and evil.

Hebrews 5:12-14

Study to show thyself approved unto God, a workman that needeth not to be ashamed, rightly dividing the word of truth.

II Timothy 2: 15

Even in stress Christ provides direction, food for growth and comfort, for He has sailed all seas before us and remains to live in our hearts as a compass to point the way and a rudder to change the direction of our ways even unto this day and forever and ever. Amen!

Who Am I?

She just doesn't have a good self-image! A friend blurted out such a statement about a friend and co-worker. This event caused me to begin examining what I really thought of myself and what is the difference in having a good self-image and being self- centered to the point of having an EGO problem? Just what is a healthy level of self- esteem? Who in the world am I anyway? What does God have to say about self? The usual concept of a Christian is selflessness, a giving person to the point of non-identity almost. I do not believe this is what God wants from us, for believing in His ability to do something through us is essential to being able to help others--essential to being able to see a need and knowing that He has gifted us with at least the desire to accomplish that service. Any special talent or ability we may have is also His gift. Women today often are torn by the "Who Am I?" syndrome Women may feel guilty for not performing enough service. We think "I am daughter to my parents, I owe them for what they gave me." True, the Bible says, "Honor thy father and thy mother."

Why that is even the first commandment with promise! And "My husband works so many hours and really doesn't like to write--and the children why have them, if I can't at least attempt to be the best mother in our neighborhood. And it isn't fair that my poor husband has to work so many hours. I really should go back to work at least part time to make ends meet." Or "My family and my husband and I have invested so much in my education, don't I owe it to everyone to follow the career I trained for? There never seems to be enough time and energy to do all I really SHOULD do!"

Intensity grows and grows until suddenly, because it has built silently, a woman often begins to think, "Hey, when do I ever get to be me? When do I ever get to just devote a little time and effort to myself?"

Actually men are not exempt from these feelings, for he may be torn between, "All I seem to be good for around here is just to bring home the paycheck and to carry out the garbage! What kind of life is that?" and "I can't even make enough money to pay the bills and now my wife is wanting to go back to work. What kind of man am I, anyway?"

We all have identity problems at times. Sometimes it seems that we expect more of ourselves than God expects of us. Oh, no, the scenario above serves to demonstrate that we often expect different things of ourselves than God expects. What does God want with human beings anyway? We are, after all, weak, unfaithful, and unpredictable among other things. I like the quotation of playwright Eugene O'Neill, "Man is born broken. He lives by mending. And the grace of God is the glue." What better bonding agent is there? Genealogy and the fascination with roots and heritage is intriguing. Although I am a history/biography devotee, I can still see that few of us have proper claim to nobility in our background and yet there is another sense in which that is not true. A Christian can justifiably shout, "I'm the child of the King!" When we feel at our lowest ebb, stretched far beyond endurance, that fact offers comfort and challenge.

WHO AM I? WHOSE?

No Lord have I save one,
No Master save He.
In submission, I stand tall,
But not alone.
Yea, then I stand in a strength,
An ability that is not mine.

I know not the how or the why,
But the WHO I know.
"I am that I am," said He
That is WHOSE I am.
Knowing this, all other identity
And seeking after ego is senseless.
When the "WHOSE I am" is settled
The "who I am" is clear.
I am His.

Yet a little while and the world seeth me no more; but ye see me; because I live, ye shall live also. At that day ye shall know that I am in my Father and ye in me, and I in you. John 14:19-20

Greater love hath no man than this, that a man lay down his life for his friends. Ye are my friends, if ye do whatsoever I command you. Henceforth I call you not servants; for the servant knoweth not what his lord doeth; but I call you friends for all things that I have heard of my Father I have made known unto you. Ye have not chosen me, but I have chosen you. John 15:13-16.

The phrase translated "in me" is literally En Theos...in God. That is the origin of the word "enthusiasm." Limp and lifeless attitudes have no place in the Christian life, for belonging to God places each of us --En Theos, in God. There is a dear old hymn my Grandmother Coffey used to sing endlessly as she scrubbed clothes on the rub board in rural Oklahoma. As a small child I did errands for her so I could beg her to tell me family tales of filing claim in southwestern Oklahoma Territory or of my Great-grandmother Virginia Tennessee McDaniel Yell and her antics as a child during the Civil War. "I am a stranger here within a foreign land...I'm here on business for my King." That sense of identity became an expectation which became real when I gave my heart and life to "King Jesus". I am constantly overwhelmed and somewhat baffled at the preciousness of the regard God the Father, the Son and the Holy Spirit places upon His own. The following scriptures explain it far better than I ever could.

But ye are a chosen generation, a royal priesthood, a holy nation, a peculiar people; that ye should show forth the praises of Him who hath called you out of darkness into His marvelous light. I Peter 2:9

For God who commanded the light to shine out of darkness hath shined in our hearts, to give the light of knowledge of the glory of God in the face of Jesus Christ. II Corinthians 6:14

He that hath an ear, let him hear what the Spirit saith unto the churches. to him that overcometh will I give to eat of the hidden manna, and will give him a white stone, and in the stone a new name written, which no man knoweth saving he that receiveth it. Revelation 2:17

Oh the depth of the riches both of wisdom and knowledge of God! How unsearchable are His judgments, and His ways past finding out! Romans 11:33

Awesome! In the joy and knowledge that we are His children, there is also need for the warning, "Be not wise in our own conceits." It is easy at times to become filled with pride and self righteousness because of our amazement at being a Christian, but Peter in his first epistle chapter 5 verse 5 warns:..........Be clothed with humility: for God resisteth the proud, and giveth grace to the humble.

NO WAY, MAN

Philosophize your way to heaven?
No way, man!
God's wisdom confounds the world's wise.
No man can learn enough or think enough
To elevate himself
To any measure of merit.
In whom do you find wisdom?
"What man among you by taking thought
Can add one cubit to his stature?"
No way, man.

Work your way to heaven?
No way, man.
Serve man to gain favor with God?
No, rather serve because you belong to Him.
"Your righteousness is as filthy rags."
But "a broken and contrite heart,
God will not despise."
Merit salvation by works?
No way, man!
Buy your way to heaven?
No way, man!
Redemption is not for sale.
Filthy rags have no market value.
But payment has already been made
By Jesus Christ
God's Son Savior.
No other way, man!

The Master in His wisdom, works, and wealth
Takes man's surrendered will and from weakness
Creates miraculous power.

Then is man elevated to the level of God?
No way, man!
What a paradox!
Only when a man becomes a trusting bond slave,
Sold out to God
Is he called by Christ Jesus,
"Friend and Brother," for
An elevated, glorified Christ
Draws all men unto Him.
No other WAY, man!

Jesus saith unto him, "I am the Way, the Truth, and the Life, no man cometh unto the Father but by Me." John 14:6

There is an old hymn which declares, "There's a new name written down in glory, and it's mine!" It extols the joy of salvation and refers to the special precious relationship each has in heaven. Names mean something, I remember vividly a low point in my emotional strength when my doctor told me, "Just remember, you are a survivor!" I gasped, for suddenly I knew, "No, I am VICTORIOUS. That is the meaning of my Irish maiden name, Coffey." As added reassurance I realized that even my given name means strong, robust. (If you could see me you would know how well that name fits me!) How like us not to live up to our inheritance. I am a big person. Even that bigness gives me added responsibility to live up to.

Like the student who turned his blessings into burdens in the STRESS chapter, we, too, are to be faithful in that small thing that we might be made ruler over many. As a Christian, he was and is a partaker of eternity, so are we. We must not deny our inheritance.

PARTAKER OF ETERNITY

Man is a wisp; a vapor.
God is eternal, everlasting, forever.

When man's will bows to the will of God
In acceptance of the Savior,
This vapor then takes on substance,
Becomes a joint-heir with Christ
And a child of God.
Mortal becomes immortal.
And a partaker of eternity.

Come, buy eternal food without price.
Partake, for God has abundantly provided.
Isaiah 55:1

A student came to me years ago requesting help in finding sources to do a philosophy paper on Jesus as a philosopher. I said, "I can find material in several sources such as the ENCYCLOPEDIA OF RELIGION AND ETHICS, but that I didn't consider Him merely a philosopher." She looked at me intently for a moment and then she said with a mixture of awe and bewilderment, "Oh, I see! Put a man up against another, big deal! Measure a man by Jesus' example, and.........." Some time after that encounter with the student, I wrote the following poem.

CALL ME THEOPHILUS

How does one measure man?
Height and breadth and weight,
Wealth, success, power, prestige,
Merit, motive or values?

Give me a tall heart that cares,
One that stretches out to the stricken world
And weighs as heavily as the sorrow of Christ,
Give me a heart light with joy
And promise of heaven!

Golden streets and jasper are my inheritance,
But the richness of here and now are mine also.
Is a child of the King lacking
In success, power and prestige?
As for merit, motive or values--
God is the Judge, the Giver of law.
All true means of measuring are His.

How does one measure me?
How does one measure nothing?
My only plea is, "Call me Theophilus.
One who loves God.

The Lord seeth not as man seeth; for man looketh on the
outward appearance, but the Lord looketh on the heart.
I Samuel 16:7

And He saith unto them, "Ye are that which justify yourselves
before men; but God knoweth your hearts:
for that which is highly esteemed among men is
abomination in the sight of God.
Luke 16:15

Society today seems constantly in search of a "meaningful re-
lationship." Now what in the world does that mean in a spiritual
sense? Given the scriptures above it seems almost impossible, but
provision has been made.

MY FATHER

How do I relate to God who created universes?
Who stretched galaxy upon galaxy in space?
Man on the moon staggers my imagination!

"In the beginning God," said a voice from space
Affirming what every spiritual man finds evident,
But man's accomplishments, as
Astounding as they seem, have reached only
To the first limited inch in God's creation.
Could it be that even the moon-walks are
A form of man's search for God,
A quest, age old and constant until Christ comes again?

Stand still for a moment, man.
God's vision is better than ours.
He knows where we are, for He is here as well as there.
God's gift of faith is the only means to open our eyes.
To give us a glimpse of Him.

Father, how do you contend with us,
So impetuous, impatient, stumbling?
And yet Your loving kindness is constantly evidenced
In regeneration and in all creation.
Our Father, thank you.

Pondering my relationship to God and his creation gives me no real excuse to plead ignorance, to shrug my shoulders and claim no responsibility for my actions or their impression of me, my example before them. Who am I? A child of Light, a child of God, joint-heir with Jesus and responsible before God for my actions.

Unaware

"And she claims to be a Christian! How can she say she is a Christian and treat people the way she does? Do you think she REALLY is?" The person seated across from me was of another race and cultural background. There are very few evangelical Christians in her country of origin. My visitor was not being catty, but she was genuinely troubled and struggling to understand. It was known from personal observation that I had been among those on the receiving end of "the treatment" and that I knew the Lord. I could not truthfully pretend I did not know what she was talking about without both failing the Lord and betraying the trust my visitor was showing me.

I must honestly admit I was sorely tempted to let my tongue become a pair of scissors and cut the subject of discussion into tiny pieces. Somehow caring for the person across from me seemed more needful and satisfying than vengeance for wrongs real or imagined, observed or unobserved.

Without really thinking, I found myself using a parable as an answer to her questions. "Some time ago when a certain high public official was running for election, I was subjected to some good-natured teasing by my fellow librarians who knew-- 1. that he was of the same denomination as I and 2--that I probably would not vote for him because of my supposed (although unspoken) political persuasion. This little dilemma or test amused them, for it meant I seemingly must be less than charitable and criticize a prominent person who made a public claim to Christianity.

To their surprise, I said instead, "I can't judge the man; that is not my responsibility anyway. I'll just say this: You can slap any label on any old bottle, but it's what's on the inside that counts." It wasn't the answer they expected, but that's the only answer I could give then and the only answer I give you now." I smiled and leaned back in my chair.

A knowing smile played across my visitor's lips. The original question was no longer germane, for we both agreed that it was up to God to make things right. The title Judge is His and not mine; that is indisputable. Vengeance does not belong to anyone else. As the door closed behind her, tears came to my eyes, for hanging on the wall of my office I saw the poem God gave me about ten years before entitled CHILD OF LIGHT. I kept it there to remind me that pretense and hypocrisy are ever-present traps awaiting me and all of us who profess the name of Jesus. I had ministered to my visitor, but somehow I had never been able to feel at peace in my dealings with the subject of discussion. Shortly after that visit of a friend and co-worker seeking my opinion, God gave me the poem below.

UNAWARE

How often have I met you, Lord,
On the streets of Denver
And failed to recognize
In those haunted, hollow eyes
An opportunity to serve?

How often in the haughty,
Abusive taunt of a Dean's demands,
Perhaps even spouting Your word at me
In self-righteous plans?

How often have I met You
In the plaintive sigh of a student
"I don't know where to begin,"
And wearily, vaguely answered,
Fourth row of indexes about the middle?"

How often within the safety, Lord,
Of my home's four walls
Has my silence built a barrier,
Failed to open a door?
---Or more?

Forgive me, Lord,
I didn't know that was You.

Laodicea! Oh, God,
How I fear that name!
Having much goods
Manufacturer and world supplier of eye salve,
And yet lukewarm, blind, unclothed
And unaware..........!

To him that knoweth to do good, and doeth it not, to him it is sin. James 4:17

People often brag, "I can read him or her like a book!" Aware or unaware we do have audiences, those who watch us with approval, those who watch with criticism, those who watch with puzzlement and so on. While we shudder at the thought of George Orwell's Big Brother, watcher, there have been watchers before and beyond the type he mentions in the book 1984. Given the technological capabilities of today even Orwell's imaginings are tame.

Each of us has a responsibility to those who watch when we know and when we do not know. I had a strange and vivid experience in that regard my freshman year in college. My new roommate and I were just getting settled in our dormitory quarters; she had gone down to get a mop and bucket from the janitor's closet. I heard a knock on our door and opened it to find a very blonde and dimpled young woman. "Are you Charlene Coffey?" she asked. When I replied that I was, she chatted for a moment with me and then finally she said, "I have been dating_____(She mentioned a high school classmate of mine.) for about a year and a half and he talks about you all the time. "I just wanted to see whether you are real. I guess you are!" Without another word she left. While I liked that classmate very much, I had no idea I would ever be subject of conversation between him and a girlfriend from a neighboring school.

Years later when things were rough for him and he was in the service my Mother let me know, for I was away at the University. I wrote him a breezy, friendly, hopefully encouraging letter. His reply amazed me, for he asked me, "I wonder whether you really realize how much you and your family mean to me?" He had never had a meal in our home, I had never dated him. It means that individuals are not going to hire cheer-leaders with pom-poms or banners to say, "Hey, I'm watching you and what you do or don't do has an influence on me for good or bad!" I honestly did not know I had that particular audience over a long period of time. Some audiences view you or you view them for seconds.

My husband and I were driving through Missouri. As we often did, we were listening to gospel music on the car radio. Ahead of us on the freeway was a recent model car with a university sticker across the back windshield, luggage in the back seat and two college-aged women in the front seat. This I observed as I was singing heartily along with the radio as was my husband. The song was "I Am Bound For the Promised Land. I am bound for the Promised Land. Oh, who will come and go with me I am bound for the Promised Land!" As we pulled up even with their car on this multi-lane highway, I looked over into the faces of the young driver and her companion. They, too, were singing, "Oh, who will come and go with me; I am bound for the Promised Land!"

It was difficult to describe adequately the looks of surprise, affirmation, kinship, and joy that passed between the occupants of those two cars traveling along across Missouri. It is enough to say that the radio was ministering to each group. Then suddenly, unexpectedly we were ministering to each other encouraging each other. Although we had never met we could recognize in that instant, a brother and sisters.

There is a sense in which as traveler, or example and warning is essential to other spiritual "travelers". We can not escape responsibility for influence we exercise on others. By omission or commission our influence is felt. Because He is and came to be our example, our salvation, choice is inescapable. Either we are His or we are not, the choice is ours, the decision is mine individually. Because as a child of eleven I gave my life to Jesus under a brush arbor next to a small church building in southwestern Oklahoma, I bear the responsibility which seemed to grip so many around me. I wondered at the simplicity of my faith and commitment and how everyone around me seemed to be questioning everything I valued. How could I hope to help these people? I found them utterly baffling at times and yet they commanded my compassion and my love!

CONFRONTATION WITH CHRIST

Confrontation with Christ,
This is the challenge of choice.
Christ never subverts the human will,

But choose we must!
There is no road around
Confrontation with Christ,
But forced submission is not His way---
Only voluntary surrender of my life
To the Way, the Truth and the Life.

This is a one way road
If you are not going with God,
Make a U-turn, brother!

There is a way which seemth right unto man, but the end thereof are the ways of death. Proverbs 41: 12

Jesus saith unto him, "I am the Way, the Truth, and the Life: No man cometh unto the Father, but by Me. Follow thou Me." John 14:16 21-22

During the Vietnam War and the unrest on campus I have mentioned, testing of faith and patriotism was extreme at times, but I was determined neither to compromise principles nor antagonize harsh feelings. Now how do you do that? I have to admit I really did not know. I determined that insofar as possible I would love each individual especially students. One day unrest had grown to such a feverish point that a one-day workshop or seminar on exploring political and social issues would displace regular class sessions. Study groups worked on selected topics. Each group selected a bibliographer to gather materials for study and discussion.

A classroom faculty member sent one such "bibliographer" to me for assistance. Their topic was "Peace in Vietnam NOW." (no ifs ands or buts). Obviously the parenthetical phrase is mine! With a mischievous smile, I asked the young man whether I wanted to prove what he already thought or did he really want to explore the subject? I assured him that I could provide resources for either stance he chose. He looked at me a little puzzled and then he said he just wanted to go down the list of peace points drawn up by a group in Boulder. I said, "Okay, but big deal!"

Without waiting for him to respond, I hastily apologized by saying, "I'm sorry. I am trying to put on you the responsibility I feel as a librarian and bibliographer for the whole college to provide all sides of every topic I can. Come on over here in the book stacks and look at the spines of these books. Don't touch any yet, just read the titles on the jackets at first!"

He gasped when he saw how many volumes we owned on his topic in our new and relatively small new college library. "I did not dream you'd have this much--"

"See, just by reading the titles alone you can almost invariably guess the political stance of the author. I'd have to be schizo-phrenic to agree with all of these writers, but I bought them all, so you'd have a chance to see things from every angle. I'll go away now and let you choose what you want to check out for your group." I gave him another mischievous grin and said, "You see I don't want to get the big head if you take a wide variety of titles and I certainly don't want to be tempted to be mad at you if you don't--Because it really isn't any of my business. But, oh, say, since I've already meddled this much--could I ask you a favor although I have no right to--would one member of your group go out to Fitzsimmons Army Hospital and talk to some of the patients out there? They are college age, too, you know!"

He ducked his head and said, "I am ashamed; I never would have thought of that!" I said in a quiet voice, "I have to admit the only reason I thought of it is that my pastor just recently baptized by immersion two young Vietnam veterans both of who lost legs in service. Truth hits with hard punches some times."

With a choked throat I left the student in the book stacks. Neither of us were likely to forget our little encounter for quite some time. Sometimes I can manage contact on an uniquely one on one basis and sometimes I seem to be utterly crippled, deaf, dumb and blind. I have yet to resolve WHY in my own mind.

Visibility because of position is sometimes an unexpected opportunity. Just by being, reputation precedes us. On the urban campus I mentioned before, we were in scattered rented locations. The White Mule Bar was on the corner of the block where the Library was built. I took a great deal of teasing when a XXX rated movie house remodeled the building on the other corner of that block, just two doors down from the Library. I made remarks to my peer faculty acquaintances like, "Oh, well, I respect our students, they'll find their way beyond those places to the Library any way!"

What they did not know was that I had walked around that building a few times praying that it could not possibly succeed financially, that it would fold. Some months after it opened it closed. By then the Library had already outgrown its quarters and we needed space for technical processes. We investigated the possibility of renting about two-thirds of that building's becoming part of the Library. While studying the space needs and remodeling plans to make the best use of that space, I discovered the records of the XXX rated movie house in a dusty pile. They would have had to have 600 attendees daily to have made a go of the business. The way the theater was divided into strange little private black booths made it next to impossible to have that many people in there during a theater day.

My prayers were answered before I said them, before they even opened for business! Again teasing began when the former XXX rated movie house became an annex to the Library. One of my classroom faculty friends asked whether I had exorcised the place before we moved in. I could legitimately tease back, "The interior used to be black and now it is painted white. What do you think? He laughed for he had anticipated my answer.

I can tell you these events, but honesty demands that I examine in my own heart potential opportunities to be of service of which I was ignorant, unwilling to acknowledge or ignored through laziness, neglect or blindness. Being unaware of need can become sin. Balance dictates that each of us take a long hard look at the potential of our lives. Being a "Light Holder" is a mission to which each Christian is called. The Lord warned about putting our light under a bushel. Admittedly, it is often uncomfortable to be seen, to have an audience aware or unaware of that role at the time; it is an essential attribute of a Christian--being an example before men for the Lord. We have come full circle and are back to the question Who am I? WHOSE? Am I a "Child of Light?"

What? know ye not that your body is the temple of the Holy Ghost which is in you, which ye have of God, and ye are not your own? For ye are bought with a price; therefore glorify God in your body, and in your spirit, which are God's. I Corinthians 6:19-20

She sighed and smoothed the manuscript before her, remembering a popular soap opera's theme song which declares sweetly: "Only love can save the world." repeatedly, but it stops short of affirming in characterization or story line that God is Love. The world is more likely to declare that "love" is God.

She remembered the example of a fellow Christian faculty member, a southern gentleman professor who was being accosted by a large "Black Panther" student, threatening and shouting in an attempt to get his grade adjusted upward. He stood his ground while other faculty entrapped in the suite of offices hid quietly. He assured the student he had assigned him the grade he had earned. This brought on louder shouts and threats. Softly the professor said calling his name, "You may out-yell me, but you can't out-love me!" Startled, the student turned on his heel and left the office suite.

Immediately a big tall work study student with long fire red curly hair came to mind. He was faithful to report to work in the library when he was scheduled nights. She was disturbed when she learned he was in the county jail. He sent word to his supervisor that he needed someone to bring his textbooks and that he felt compelled to read his Bible. Finally his trial date arrived. His direct supervisor and her supervisor asked whether she could do anything for him. She had called his public defender to ask whether character witnesses would help. He said to have everyone show up in court and that they would be called to speak in his behalf if needed.   The judge asked him to stand. She said, "Young man. It is a fortunate individual who has even one friend. It is obvious you have more than one. You are to enroll for your classes next term. And don't you blow it!" Love stands on two hind legs. The last time we saw him he was married and had a red haired little boy riding on his hip. Love often is its own reward.

Mony

Stacks of letters, complicated forms and mountains of paperwork demanded payment. Mony is how she chose to spell the word, for it seemed always short. Although both her daughter and the business officer gave help, it was still a frequent hassle which invariably arrived in Friday afternoon's mail which could not be resolved until next week. .

You do not have to pay this amount, but you do owe this if---Insurance is a necessary mixed blessing. Sometimes it was quick sand. She was thankful for the forethought which caused her to buy long term care insurance and not to rely totally on Medicare and supplemental insurance through her career retirement account. It meant paying mony up front and wondering what percentage insurance would actually deliver. Yes, MONY was the proper spelling of the word. Cash is a four letter word, but mony seem more appropriate.

She was not able to draw social security, for she had worked for the state during her career. Her husband's retirement and work history was predominately for the federal government, so even that avenue was blocked to her. If she filed for those funds she was told that her own retirement annuity would be reduced dollar for dollar as would her husband's survivors' benefit. She looked around the dining room and at different activities and wondered who among the residents were on Medicaid, meaning they had to have spent down all their assets to the level for basically burial expenses and were to live on a very limited budget of maybe $50, for shampoo and other necessities. Because of her conservative views of the economy, she could not help thinking and wondering whose inheritance she had enhanced with her tax mony's support and how often that person actually visited the resident in question. Oh, well, why bother to judge? That was between them and their own conscience. But a little digging revealed that she was one of 20 or less in the whole facility who were in the "private pay" category! This view came from having grown up in the cotton patch during dust bowl days with tight-fisted hard working parents who did not readily take any government handouts including the corduroy clothes distributed to school kids out on the farm. "I'll take care of you." her Daddy had said to explain his refusal of offered help. Thank goodness for the good old treadle Singer sewing machine and a Mother who kept it humming. Imagine a new school dress for the price of a spool of thread and an empty chicken feed sack!

She remembered an uncle having sent two huge boxes of clothes to her family unannounced from his California home. They had obviously been selected by the Salvation Army staff or something, for most items were of questionable use. None of the trousers were the correct size for the father, but the mother cut them down to make Sunday School pants for the little brothers. The scraps were turned into quilt blocks in heavy warm covers against winter's cold. Tie-tacking is a wonderful skill. There was one evening gown made of rust colored chiffon and a light dusty blue satin bed jacket edged with a feathery soft blue eider down border.. These gave her hours of imaginary adventures when she brought them out from the box under the iron bedstead to play and dream away. Money is not everything.

One day her roommate at the center had said as she entered the room, "I want an ice cream cone!" when she saw her and her daughter sharing an ice cream treat. The daughter had felt bad when she heard that remark until she told her that her roommate had just come from the ice cream social in the dining room. It was the family companionship which was more desired than the ice cream cone.

The resident council had had a Nacho fund raiser to meet the need for "goodies" for those whose families did not or could not supply them, but there are holes that even such thoughtfulness can not fill. This explained why the roommate followed every move the daughter made each visit.

Once when she was visiting family on the farm her frugal money managing father said in a thoughtful, remembering mood, "Sometimes I fear I gave you kids the wrong idea about the importance of money." She and her brother seated at the dinner table gasped. She waited for her brother to respond. When he did not, she said, "But Daddy, that isn't what came across to me. I learned that as long as I could move a muscle to do something to make things better, it was my job. If I had honestly done all I could do and it wasn't solved, then it was no longer my job." Having lots of money can't really solve everything.

One still has to pay taxes on prizes "given free" on game shows. There is no such thing as a free lunch. Somebody has to pay. She resented being called middle class by politicians who were eager to be seen as heroes. "No matter how much or how little money I have, I always retain the right to FIRST CLASS." she thought. "I've earned it. And it is called RESPECT."

An Old Testament quotation from the book of Haggai 1:5-7 came to mind. "Consider your ways. Ye have sown much, and bring in little; ye eat, but have not enough; ye drink, but ye are not filled with drink; ye clothe you, but there is none warm; and he that earneth wages earneth wages to put it into a bag with holes. Thus saith the Lord of hosts; consider your ways."

A raise in pay from 67 cents an hour to 72 cents for the graduate assistants in Library School popped into her mind! The whole class had declared that cause for celebration, abandoned the cataloging lab and headed for the student union building for an ice cold Coke. She had allowed her landlady to paint the apartment while she visited her family. She discovered that she was going to graduate mid-term and she didn't want to have an empty apartment, so she evicted her. The young painter was annoyed at her for that stunt, so he not only told her about a tiny one bedroom doll house he had just painted, he offered his truck so she could move immediately. The rent was $37.50 a month about the same as the apartment which only had a sleeping porch. Some friends are worth more than money. Time certainly changes things, but whatever the timing "MONY" remains a valid spelling..

This thought triggered a memory about wanting to buy a black patent leather purse and standing there pleadingly beside her Mother who held her cotton pulling money in trust. It had a beautiful golden chain handle and clasp and was actually a ladies' evening purse. She was a big over-grown pre-teen just learning about money and managing it. Her Mother agreed that it was a beautiful purse and looked good in her right hand's grasp. Then she said these words of wisdom. "I always thought when I bought a purse I ought to have something left to put in it." How could she argue with that?

LIFE LESSON: GOAL MEANS MORE THAN GOLD.

Boss

"I'm the line leader," she had heard her young grandson say. She chuckled remembering his proud, insistent words to his brother and sisters. Kindergarten teaches sharing, but it also teaches structure and order. A part of each of us wants and expects to be the boss on occasion.

Her Daddy had said, "Being the boss is not always what it is cracked up to be! You have to do your own job and then you still have to pull up the slack for everybody else." In the cotton patch his orders were: "Heads down and tails up!" Stooping, pulling cotton and dragging a heavy sack made her appreciate seeing the sky when she stood up. It made her appreciate using the wages for some things she wanted or needed with her parent's approval. Ah, the difference in want and need was a crucial life lesson and earning permission to spend what was earned, to be her own boss even in small things was a longed for goal.

She learned that people in authority are not always fair or considerate. At eight years of age she had been fitted for glasses to correct near-sightedness. It made seeing the chalkboard so much easier and always as a tall kid in the classroom she was seated in the back. By age 11 she was in need of new lenses. There had been no place to carry or protect her glasses while working in the field or milking cows, doing all sorts of things around the farm or at school. When the doctor saw how scratched up they were, he threw a fit and tossed them in the trash can. "You don't deserve glasses!" he snarled. "You don't treat them right!" She had stood there and trembled in anger and shame. She reached down in the trash can and snagged her old glasses. They had been paid for; they were hers not his to throw away.

She marched out into the waiting room to join her mother who asked, "Don't you need new ones?" She said that she guessed not and started out the door. It was not until she was 16 that she got new ones. Dr. S. was his own boss she thought, but he was not a very good one.

Then she remembered working for a neighbor chopping cotton with two younger brothers without their parents. The neighbor had scolded them because the 6 year old who had begged to earn money and agreed to work for half wages, was only carrying one row instead of two which she and the older brother were. She had spoken up to tell the neighbor that they were watching to see that he did a good job and put him between them to check his work. Then she added that if he took two rows, then he deserved full wages. When the neighbor paid them off he had teased their Dad that he had a good crew even if the foreman was a girl! That was interesting, bosses have bosses.

When she had received her teaching certificate and was hired by a small rural school, the superintendent of schools would give her a small budget if she took on responsibility for the library, too. She spent her free time during the state teacher's conference in a second hand book store selecting books for the library. Some were for as little as ten cents. She spent about $160. Next week back at school entered a fast talking encyclopedia salesman into the superintendent's office. When he left, the remainder of her budget was gone by a stroke of his pen. Bosses are not always truthful, honorable.

Somehow this reminded her of her then kindergarten grandson who was bright and very active. The teacher called him by name and said that if he couldn't sit still in class he could just go down to the principal's office. He said, "Oh, Okay!" As if to say, any thing is better than this! He headed down the hall toward the school office. Teachers are bosses. That is hard, responsible work and discipline is the hardest skill to master.

She remembered her parents and how they got along, how they managed a household of five children—4 boys and a girl. Daddy managed the money. Daddy was the boss. They grew up knowing that. When she was grown, her Mother was just recounting their past a bit for her. She said, "You know, I just never actually locked horns with your Daddy, but when I really, really wanted something, it just –HAPPENED. Sometimes bosses are sweet, silent, strong, invisibly so.

The summer of 1965 was a landmark time, for she returned to work after spending time with her small children. She met her new boss-to-be in the state Senate chamber offices. She was interviewed for a faculty position in the Library of Metropolitan State College which was in the process of being created. The Academic Dean who interviewed her became the ultimate concept of what a boss should be. He was a past master of working with people with honesty and respect. He was plain spoken and a consummate horse trader. When he named her head librarian she told him about her four young children and said straight forwardly, but with a tease in her voice, "Eight hours a day is all you get, old buddy, because if I fail in that job I've had it!"

He surprised her by saying, "It's always been enough as far as I can tell." Confidence and support, advice and genuine friendship, he epitomized. It did not hurt that he was also a native Oklahoman; they tend to understand each other. When she had professional questions and problems and solutions which she laid honestly before him, he would say, "Sounds good to me and WE will just…." He never made her feel stupid or weak and never let her feel a lack of support. Of course, the whole faculty was in a building mode. That should be the attitude of every organization, building even in hard times.

What did she do when she was the boss, became the question? Honesty, fairness, straight forwardness, find the very best person for the job and expect them to do it. Learn from good examples. Say what you mean and mean what you say. Find each person's strengths and encourage them to grow. Then add persons who will complement, strengthen the others. Be approachable to every person on staff. She could not claim always to have lived up to her own expectations.

She once had a boss who would not know the truth if it walked right up and bit her on the bottom. To complicate matters she often drank her lunch. She lied constantly to maintain power and the second in command had promised her if ever she did not agree with her she would resign. This position was meant to support and advocate for the staff and she had sold her soul before she even got started. The big boss lied and manipulated. She thought nothing of slaughtering good people to stay in power. Once the resident had left her position she went to the boss' boss and said, "If you want any creditability on campus whatsoever, get rid of her." To her surprise he said breathlessly. "I'm trying. I'm trying!" She was soon gone, but after she had created much chaos.

Power politics is tricky business. That is why she hated such "reality shows" as Big Brother and Survivor. Liars are plentiful enough without training sessions. Integrity is a perfectly valid trait.

Finally she came to the conclusion that self discipline is the very best boss. "Now to convince everyone else!" She said to herself with a chuckle. Two favorite quotations came to mind: The Quaker saying, "All people are a little queer except thee and me. And sometimes I question thee." And her Mother's oft repeated saying, "Other people's children!"

Evaluation demanded that she look at supervisors here in the center. How did they rate as a boss? Some were stiff and arrogant at times, but the most effective bosses did everything as it was needed. Nothing was beneath them when it stood in the way of safety, comfort, progress. They weren't too good to do any lowly task. Staff responded to example! Oh, they were vocal when a staff member slacked off, but the welfare of individual residents came first even to the point of cajoling a wayward resident into doing what was needful for the good of all. Self confidence is paramount. A boss can make the whole day for a resident by something as simple as a touch on the shoulder or moving a chair from the way of a walker.

Yes, she decided self discipline is the very best boss if your own compass is true. In the words of the Old Testament prophet, "Consider your ways."

Pain/Care

It was much better this time, but the first stay in the center was dismal, even dangerous. Extremely painful blood clots lodged in her left groin making it impossible to walk without wanting to scream at the top of her lungs. A trip to the hospital and transfer to the care center followed. A very hostile head nurse and a loud-mouthed CNA made the whole experience more painful than necessary. In putting her in the lift-to-stand the CNA had screamed right in her face. "How much do you weigh?"

Shocked and angry she asked, "Can't you even read a chart?" Just then a massive bleed filled the floor with black liquid. The last thought she remembered with the wet sticky substance streaming down her legs into her shoes and onto the floor was: "Well good. Now you have to clean it up!"

Her daughter had just left that night, but was haunted by an uneasy feeling which made her return. In the meantime she was cleaned up and put to bed unaware of what was really going on. When her daughter came back in, she learned that they could get no blood pressure reading after three tries by the duty nurse. No call to the daughter or son had been made. Upon her unexpected return, the staff member asked the daughter whether she wanted to call any other member of the family to keep watch with her. Then she asked how old the resident was and said, "Oh, that is the age my mother was when she died."

The daughter said, "No. She is going to the hospital right now!" She had told her later that she had looked like wax and no one seemed to have a clue. After a trip to the emergency room and surgery to repair the internal tear, she had recovered enough to be returned to the center. The original CNA was no where to be found then. No one would discuss what had happened. The head nurse disappeared off the scene also. Her own career had involved recruiting and supervising personnel. She became more vocal and "pleasantly" demanding as she recovered and energy and awareness returned. Family was even more alert also. It is so important to have family visits. Residents are not always capable of speaking for themselves.

Physical therapy followed. At that time it seemed to be the only personal attention given. A physical therapist even started coming in to work early to get her out of bed. Only one person in physical therapy seemed to care enough to acknowledge her existence. Meals were brought to the bedside with minimal attention paid to how, or whether food was eaten. Food offered was mostly starchy and poorly prepared. Through persistent and sometimes patient trickery on the part of the re-hab staff person, she learned to walk again. Toileting was pretty much ignored. Meds, lack of real exercise and fiber in the diet made BMs misery. Frequent presence of a family member helped immeasurably to improve attentiveness to care. Change and upgrading of personnel improved care somewhat. Reasonable work load and quality and level of staffing is crucial. An occasional thank you to the proper persons does not hurt either.

Down the hall a woman lay on her bed talking to herself, endlessly repeating, "I told you I love you." over and over. She knew that the resident got out of bed only once a day for a while.

She had been an art teacher at some point in her life and then reportedly there was an auto crash or was it MS, rumors run the gambit in a population such as this. Her care took some skilled handling. Family came and went, but there was no real opportunity to develop a friendship, for her mental state and sanctioned contact did not permit it. All meals were taken in bed and the only freedom was on shower day and a short time in her wheelchair. She noticed that one CNA was especially skillful handling her. Continuity of staffing would help, she observed to herself. "If I were running the show--"

Across the hall one woman was so demanding of attention and staff time that her care was a detriment to caring for others. She wanted to be slathered with lotion multiple times especially after showers and wanted her shower scheduled late at night which conflicted with bedtime schedules for most of the other residents. Her roommate seemed to feed off her needs and wanted in on the special treatment. She could not help but wonder why the center did not demand that the family arrange for a constant care giver, but then there was apparently no funds for such one on one care and no reasoning with the individual. No one had taught her the concept of sharing as a child, or maybe she was just being a child all over again.

A comb-over attempted to cover the scar on the skull of a man who had had brain surgery, leaving him paralyzed on one side. He used a huge, bulky wheelchair with a tray attached. She noticed that he patted that hand constantly as if to reassure himself that it was still there. His surgery left him sight impaired on one side. This coupled with the need for extending one foot on a rest, triggered impacts with other wheelchairs in the dining room and hallway traffic. Add all this to a very restless, impatient, roaming spirit, irritation was frequent, but he is personable at times and loved board games and sports on TV. Patience is a virtue hard to come by.

Home

The CNA on duty tucked the roommate in for the night. Immediately she let out a wail, "I want to go home." She was annoyed by the noise, for she had just fallen asleep. "Quiet, Please" she said in a loud demanding tone, for the roommate was deaf, sometimes selectively so. This happened frequently and was often ignored to let her tire herself out, but tonight she did not feel that tolerant. She had on one occasion asked her where was home and the roommate answered, "Brighton".

"But you are there," she was told and the roommate wailed, "No, I am not!" No amount of empathy seemed to help, so she just concentrated on the television program and the book she held in her hands once she turned on her light. .

She was reminded of the sweetness of the remarks of her then 9 year old grandson when he had learned that she was selling her large five bedroom home to move into a one bedroom apartment in a retirement community. "Grandma," he said "Wouldn't it be wonderful if when you get there it is an exact replica of here?" She said, "But I will take lots of my things and my memories and imagination. Besides all of you can come visit me." Now it was different, but only in space and having to share that space. She was reminded of the Clint Black song "Where ever you go; there YOU are!"

She remembered a young fellow faculty member had teased her about being an Okie from Muskogee. She was an Oklahoman she had said and that her roots went back to Oklahoma territory and the Cheyenne Arapahoe land opening. Then determined to get her goat he said, "So you stole Indian land? That is what Oklahoma is." She retorted, "And Manhattan isn't?"

"Oh, I knew I shouldn't argue with you." He had traveled widely and was educated in part in Austria. She liked sparring with him. Home is where the heart is. She had spent far more time in Colorado than she had in Oklahoma, but Oklahoma was still her home.

Different cultures always fascinated her. Two Afghan brothers attended Metropolitan State College and frequented the college library. One day when she was on duty at the reference desk, they, knowing that she actually headed the library, decided to challenge her.

One said with an impish grin, "In my country you would be at your home, busy taking care of your babies."

She had smiled and said, "Aren't you two lucky to be in my country and have me here to help you?" They gave a little chuckle and she had felt pleased that they were at home enough in "their/her" library they felt free to tease her. Home is where the heart is.

Eyes

If Beauty is in the eye of the beholder, so then, too, is Ugly. It is all in how you look at it. Or as Abraham Lincoln put it, "A man is about as happy as he makes up his mind to be." She looked around the floor at scattered used tissues along with chunks of cheese and crackers left behind by the roommate's night time snack. Housekeeping had not yet arrived. Reading pain and far-away memories in the eyes of fellow residents was a habitual pre-occupation.

Somehow the memory of her adult brother's remark came to mind. "All my life," he had said thoughtfully, "I have tried to anticipate what Daddy would want me to do next." She had mentally gasped, "No wonder Daddy, and therefore the family, thought of him as slow to react. He has been ahead and therefore never right on time. When she had told their father what the son had said, his reaction was: "That's the craziest thing I ever heard!" She tried to convince the father of her point of view without any success. All she could decide was, "It's all in how you look at things!"

Then she thought of her theory that the CNA staff really ran the place, because it is the CNA who answers the call buttons.

They do the work without having the policy making power to affect change. It is all in how you look at things. Administrators have training and power, but they do not always have pertinent experience to make meaningful policy changes based on individual acquaintance with needs. Oh, there are meetings for in-put, but not always eyes and ears to ascertain the true meaning. Resident council meetings are meant to be the voice of residents to address concerns, but too often decisions are an accomplished fact before residents are aware of changes.

"It's a dignity issue." often is code/statement/excuse for actions implemented. A resident said in a meeting, "Is it more dignified to wear a clothing protector or oatmeal down the front of your clothes all day? I choose the bib and I suspect the laundry would also." Even during the resident council meetings she kept hearing the echo of her library staff meetings: "The students come first!" Here it is the residents who come first, even when they are not vocal enough to be heard.

A small precise woman said to a table mate about someone at a nearby table, "She must be seven feet tall, but she is nice!" The subject of the comment swallowed a giggle and thought, "Don't you realize that I see you, too?"

Know

"Knowledge and wisdom are two entirely different things. There is such a thing as an educated fool." Her Daddy who read just about everything he could get his hands on had said that more than once. Further "BE NOT WISE IN YOUR OWN CONCEITS" the Bible admonishes. There is a vast difference in knowing and common sense--wisdom. In a discussion she and her daughter came to the conclusion not only are there two sides to every coin there is the edge of that coin and the metal it is made from. Nothing is as simple as face value, for at times other factors are to be considered and yet there is right and there is wrong.

One of her very earliest memories is of sitting in her Daddy's lap watching him read and marveling at his ability to read and the passion he had for this past time. It was then, before she could read a word of English that she vowed one day she would not only learn to read, she would read everything in the world there was to read. This was with the howling of the winds of the dust bowl and the middle of the Great Depression. A librarian in the making was born.

People being people; they are sometimes quite annoying. She

remembered coming home from school fuming to her Daddy that so and so was so mean and ornery they stink! Her Dad had caught her flat-footed by saying, "Be careful kid, you just might be smelling your own upper lip!" That and the Bible verse, "Be ye kind." often stopped her in her tracks. Wisdom? She did not like being wrong even in the smallest degree. Thinking and analyzing are hard work. Admitting truth is even harder sometimes.

She smiled and puzzled at the Quaker quotation: "All people are a little queer except Thee and Me and sometimes I question Thee." Then came a memory of her then 4 year old grand daughter's disagreement with someone who had called another "stupid". She responded, "There are no stupids in this family, only HUMANS."

"Just put it in God's hands and let go." she heard someone say, but she said to herself, "He expects us to do some things for ourselves, otherwise you are just a useless blob." And the wisdom to know the difference phrase from the Alcoholics Anonymous prayer came to mind. Getting to know others promotes patience and peace. Standing up for what is right is a dangerous move at times. Being a peacemaker is also dangerous, for the peacemaker is often caught in the middle. "Jack be nimble, Jack be quick" is a nursery rhyme with more depth than one might think. Ah, integrity and ego, where is the balance?

She chuckled under her breath upon remembering two carpentry workmen making alterations to the Library's lay-out. They were discussing women and work and included her in the discussion. She had responded to their invitation by laughingly concluding, "Don't you know that Librarians know everything!" One of them said gruffly, "Tell me about it!" What she did not realize was that one of the men was recently divorced. His ex-wife was a Librarian. Knowing ones audience helps!

A teen memory of her Mother came to mind when she was standing before the mirror on the dresser with a pair of scissors in hand. She was clipping little sprigs of gray hair along a mole beside her ear. They were buried among the locks of thick rich, deep brown hair. The teen-aged daughter had said, "I won't mind having a gray haired mother, but I refuse to have a bald one." A bemused smile crossed the mother's face and she said, "I suppose it could come to that if I keep this up."

Then she remembered writing a letter to the student newspaper reporting the actions of a fictional pre-med student whose friend suffered a paper cut on his finger. The medical student could not tolerate imperfection, so he removed his friend's wounded finger which, of course, made his hand imperfect which made his arm imperfect. Soon he was left with no friend at all. Finding fault is not wisdom and should be replaced by encouragement and support whenever possible.

Long ago her first grade teacher gave her a coloring page with written instructions: Color the wagon blue. This defied reason, for all wagons worth anything were red. Her wagon was red. Surely the teacher was all mixed up. She colored her wagon red and got a big fat minus for a grade at the top of the page. The teacher did not bother to ask her why she had chosen to use red. She had been told never to "talk back to her teacher," so she said nothing in her own defense. She just tried to remember when she taught students to always ask "Why?"

Her daughters were practically born with crayons in their hands, but her son showed little or no interest in them until one day she came upon him on the floor of the laundry room on his knees. He had a newspaper near the sweeper and a green crayon in his hand in the darkened room. She asked him what he was doing. He answered, "Shhh! I am writing vacuum cleaner." He had written in large block letters H O O V E R. Until he could do the whole thing he wasn't going to bother. Everyone learns differently and at his own speed. He was four.

She remembered being approached by a professor with a doctorate requesting that she buy a book called Dr. X about a doctor accused of malpractice for their fledging college library.

She said that it was more a selection for the public library and was, in fact, a current title in their collection and so popular that they had several copies. And that it was so popular that it was on the reserve waiting list to be checked out from Denver Public Library now. He said, "Yes, but it would cost me a quarter to put my name on the reserve list!"

"So," she said, "You are asking me to spend $25.00 of the college's book budget, so you won't have to spend a quarter to reserve the book. I really must consider that!"

Later she learned that the professor had a child who was brain damaged. That simply could not be unless it was the doctor's fault. Knowledge and wisdom are two entirely different things.

As a college freshman, she had eagerly joined the newspaper staff. The faculty sponsor called her in to discuss her first submission for publication. He had liberally marked editorial changes on her "deathless prose." Then he said, "I think with a little work you just might become a writer. Two rules here, you don't cry and you don't bleed! Above all you leave your opinion for the editorial page." This gruff, experienced public relations man taught her more about writing than the professor in the all the journalism classroom lectures. Some media types today seem not to have learned that lesson.

At O. U creative writing course work was taken as an extra load when she did her graduate work in librarianship. She studied under Dr. Walter Campbell, Stanley Vestal of western history and Native American fame. He taught her that while English teachers tell students that every good sentence needs a subject or noun and an action word, a verb, he would insist that in creative writing every sentence required a fact and a feeling. Those teachings and studying the Psalms and New Testament gospels of the King James version of the Bible taught her to write. She smiled at remembering a quotation from President Dwight David Eisenhower: "An intellectual is a man who takes more words than necessary to tell more than he knows." She concluded that the right words are both the paint and the canvas in creating a written masterpiece.

Suddenly she remembered an attractive young student who came to the reference desk to request a Bible. She said, "I need to look at one." The reference librarian obliged and ask her whether she sought any particular portion of scripture. She said, "No, I just want a Bible." As the sponsor of the Baptist Student Union she often kept extra copies of the HOLY BIBLE in her office, so she offered to go get one to give her one of her own as soon as she got off desk duty. She smiled with a knowing gasp and said, "No, thanks. It is the obligation of parents to give every child a Bible. I am calling my folks." A few days later she stopped by her desk and triumphantly waved a Bible in her hand. She never did learn what was the burning urgency which drove her to want to own a Bible. Knowing and wisdom are often tied together.

Food

This second stay in the center saw the food served improve 100%, but is short of perfection. And there were the contrarians who found fault with this or that. They did not attend the monthly food committee's meeting to discuss the menu for the upcoming month.

"It's not the pot roast my mother always made!" And "How can they call this potato soup with chunks of potato this big!" Trying to please a 100 or more tastes is not the easiest thing in the world. Diabetics sneaking sugar packets has to be a source of concern also. And budget realities exist as well. One resident frequently requests that lobster be the main course for the resident planned meal of the month. Fortunately that request is voted down as a matter of choice by the group.

She welcomes chili with corn bread menus, for she always requests skim milk be served with her meals. Skim milk is most appropriate, for the family separated milk in order to sell the cream that was the family's source of income. No one is likely to know that the cornbread is treasured to become cornbread and milk in her glass. This takes her back to her grandparents' front porch for the evening ceremony of a big glass of fresh milk with a huge wedge of salty homemade cornbread. It doesn't matter that the cornbread served is sweet and in the form of a muffin. Fingers are made to crumble cornbread. Most suppers on the farm were pinto beans with thick brown broth (sometimes with and sometimes without a hambone) and sometimes potatoes on the side.

There was cornbread and beans followed by cornbread and milk. There was also green tomato chow chow or corn relish to spark up the beans which were heaped on top of the cornbread topped by beans with a smothering of thick brown juice. Often there was a generous slice of onion or pickled beets if the gardening season had had enough rain to raise the produce. Imaginary menu items were welcomed to her mind and were almost as filling and satisfying as the real thing. As her mother always said, "Appetite is the very best cook."

The center's dining room is always full and many choose room trays. Not many grumble over what is being served, at least she did not. She watched as many made eager selections. Breakfast in the dining room is her socializing time, but lunch and supper are brought to her room. She hates the wheelchair rodeo she has to endure getting to and from the dining room for meals. It represents so much lost time which could be spent writing or reading. Breakfast time is observation time. She mused that one resident could not start his day without a huge puddle of hot chocolate on the floor and a generous splashing of brown stains from shoe top to trouser leg on his white sports socks.

She smiled at remembering a very tall white haired man with a walker who led a short, very slightly built World War II vet inside the dining room. They were quite late arriving for breakfast. When they finally stood at the table next to hers, the other residents at that table had eaten and were gone. The taller of the two men said in a loud commanding voice to staff nearby who were waiting on others, "Clear this table and feed this hungry old man!" It was so comical that she had almost giggled at his demand.

He is almost the age of the smaller man and always wants to be in charge. Swiftly coffee appeared before the older man and his breakfast order taken. The taller man left to go to his own table to order two bowls of oatmeal. She then left for church services in the lobby since it was Sunday. The noon menu was roasted turkey with all the trimmings.

Almost everyone should be satisfied. Even then alternative menu selections are a pleasant choice. She was pleased to note that ice cream on demand was a choice! Or a hot dog!

Rain

Diamonds scattered across the lawn outside the Re-Hab gym. She watched the drops of moisture sparkle red, green and clear in the early morning sunshine through the glass exit doors. Robins played in the gutters along street's curb side and then they came up onto the lawn to peck hungrily on grass seed. Many of the other residents watched birds, bunnies and even red fox vixen with kits play among the ground's trees and shrubs at the end of the low brick buildings of the center. They religiously watched the weather and discussed the current weather and the forecasts. Some of them begged, borrowed stole time to tour the grounds in their wheelchairs when staff could spare the time. One mobile resident takes his wheeled walker for a daily walk to a favorite spot under a large maple tree frequented by small dark birds. He is making real progress walking with his shaky body responding to physical therapy. He makes up his own bed and lies flat of his back on the bed to shave with his cordless razor. Constantly he is a pleasant soul, rain or shine, smiling and greeting others.

Rain met with mixed reviews, but those who lived through the dust bowl days welcomed any form of moisture. Rain, snow, fog, but prolonged dark days made for subdued moods and even grumbles from some. Carl Sandburg's poem came to mind, "Fog creeps in on little cat's feet/ And then moves on." Remembering early days in Denver when her children were very small, she smiled at the memory of a surprise heavy rainfall outside their old duplex. She opened the door leading to the front porch and placed a quilt on the floor for the children to join her where they made up songs and watched the shower of bright autumn leaves fall down with the pelting raindrops. It was a special time with everyone snuggled in blankets and enjoying each other's company--making memories accompanied by their own music. She wondered what rain memories other residents had.

Early garden English peas and newly dug baby potatoes were the gifts of spring rains when she was a child and her mother made a delicious white sauce when she served them to the family. Rain meant food on the table and crops in the fall and money to church offerings. Otherwise the pastor might be paid with a fryer and canned lambs quarter weeds gathered from the spring growth along the roadside when there was no cash crop to share.

"Into each life some rain must fall." That saying raced through her mind. It was followed by remembering the proverb: "All sunshine makes a desert!" So many thoughts chased themselves through her mind, but she hesitated to share them with the other residents. So many of them seemed so closed off and "unsharing". She found that she was more likely to share her thoughts with the staff especially with CNAs and nurses or occasionally with the re-hab staff. Sometimes in Story Hour discussions triggered sharing thoughts, memories. Those times served as rainfall which produced sharing sometimes. It was then she tried to inspire/encourage residents to put their memories down on paper so they could grow and their stories would not be lost. She raced to the computer's keyboard to write them down. The raindrops flowed through her fingertips with her thoughts and memories. She realized that she was sometimes closed off, too.

She was so thankful for the rain.

Gift

Decorations indicated the anticipation of Christmas. Conversations among the staff and residents told of the rush of the season and memories of long ago Christmas seasons mixed in with plans for the upcoming one and longed for visits from relatives and friends. The true meaning of the gift of the Christ Child was sometimes interjected into the conversations and certainly during the church service, the mini-concerts and the group singing. She could not help but think of her childhood question to the Sunday School teacher, "Since it is Jesus' birthday where are our gifts for Him?" The answer was: "Giving to another and loving others is meant to be a gift to God

"Oh!"

She was thankful for the gift of imagination. She wondered what her fellow residents thought and questioned in her mind the sadness and sourness she read upon some faces. Why? What were their family backgrounds? What were their physical ailments? She wasn't exactly a Pollyanna, but she was thankful that pleasantness was her usual mood. Maybe she could pass it on.

When she was a child on a tenant farm in southwestern Oklahoma there was never a Christmas tree at their house. That was only at their school. There was no Christmas tree lot, no evergreen groves, unless you counted salt cedar bushes, and no money to buy a tree if one had been readily available. Gifts were exchanged in the family according to names drawn. She remembered one Christmas when an uncle got mixed up about which of her four brothers' name he had drawn. One brother got two gifts and one of the youngest brothers got none. Fortunately she had drawn the name of one of the youngest and had bought with her cotton pulling money a toy train made of wood and painted silver. It was a streamliner train rounded and sleek on the front as well as on the caboose. She quickly divided the four car train in half, giving each little boy two train cars. If they felt cooperative they could have a four car train to play with together or if they were in an independent mood they each had a two car train. That was the Christmas when she was 13 almost 14 and her grandmother gave her a baby doll. Her Daddy had chided his mother saying, "She is too big to be getting a doll for Christmas!"

Quietly she had leaned over to whisper to her father, "The doll is really for Grandma! She says she never in her life got enough dolls."

"Oh!" was his surprised response.

At the breakfast table at the care center, Christmas memories were shared at times. Memories of twelve children in one family who often got more food and gifts on New Year's Day than on Christmas were recounted and memories of being given a nickel or dime each or a piece of fruit. At her house New Year's Day just meant a new calendar for the year in the mail from the local bank.

Another kind of gift suddenly came to her mind and the announcement which triggered it one night beside the old Warm Morning heating stove: her intention to go to college. Her father had said, "Well, I don't know how!"

Her answer was, "I don't know either, but I AM going."

In a couple of weeks her Daddy had an announcement of his own. "You're not going to school Friday."

(This was an unheard of event, for school was mandatory in her family.) They, she and her parents, made the 70 mile trip along Route 66 to the nearest public college, Southwestern. She came back enrolled for the summer term and with a half time job in the cafeteria for her room and board. It was a gift she had not dreamed of, for her father gave permission to write a check on his account for tuition, books and supplies. At the end of each month's work she had to walk up to the business office to endorse her paycheck over to the college for her room and board. She had to work a banquet or find other income for toothpaste and other needs. Her gift was beyond belief; her brothers received a heifer and half ownership of a new Ford tractor. Her parents were fair. War Bonds finally supplied funds to buy more milk cows and cash to buy the home place from the grandfather. The whole family worked hard, but the thoughtful management of money became a gift to her and to each member of the family.

They went from tenant farm family to a dairy farm owner selling to Borden's in Amarillo, but the cotton fields remained, as well. At college the dorm residents drew names for a secret Santa. She drew the name of a fellow cafeteria worker who had just lost her father to a house fire. Their home was destroyed and she was struggling to stay in college. The challenge to select a gift and a secret surprise or two became a puzzle. For a dime she bought an oval cut glass dish and several pieces of hard Christmas candy which she left at the dormitory's office with her friend's name on it. She had the staff buzz the proper room number. Then she contacted her own Mother to ask permission to give her friend a new homemade cotton-filled quilt in a crazy quilt design. The very best gift, however, was the promise to pray for her and her family which included a mother and several younger siblings.

She was shocked to be told that God didn't have time to listen to her petty little problems. In surprised gasp she had said, "Then just what good is He?" She knew her friend attended the same church her own roommate did which was right across the street from her own church's building. When the girl had burst into tears she knew that her remark had hit home. What better gift is there than sharing God's love?

That reminded her of a first memory of the Sunday school collection plate being passed in her class. When the plate was passed at the table at home she took a helping for her own plate. Baffled she reached for the smallest coin in the collection plate --a dime. She was even more surprised to have the older girl sitting next to her take her hand in hers and squeeze until she dropped the dime back into the plate. Learning to give is a valuable lesson that has to grow in the heart.

Lost

A new man came to breakfast saying that he had been in 5 different care centers and that he really would rather be in his own place. A woman cried out across the dining room, "Sweet and Low, Coffee," and some unrecognizable phrase very loudly and repeatedly. He then repeated that he had been in all these different centers and two of the five had separate places for the "dead beats". What? What do you mean?

"Those who don't know what they are doing." Then he said, "I hope that God never lets me live that long. (She learned later he was 88.) "In one place I was in I saw a granddaughter bring in her 105 year old grandmother and just leave her. She was not that bad, but she just never came to see her. My sons say I have to stay here since I need around the clock care that they can't give me and I can't do for myself. What do I have, an 8 by 9 space shut off with curtains? The rest of the room and the bathroom is shared with a blind man who has been here for 8 years." He finished his last bite of breakfast and then said, "I'm out of here." And one of his table mates said, "Now you be good." as he wheeled away to the hallway toward his room. He said that his goal was to get into the veteran's home at Fitzsimmons. Now why would he say such a thing "dead beats!"

"As if they had a choice!" How must it feel to be that lost inside themselves to the point they did not know the persons nearest and dearest to them? How lonely and lost! Their loud outbursts were disconcerting in the middle of meals or down the hall in the middle of the night. She saw wives visit husbands and husbands visit wives who did not have the vaguest idea who held their hands and yet reached out to touch perfect strangers and to explore someone else's room and blankly ask, "Where is this?" if they spoke at all. Or they might hug a doll or stuffed animal for companionship. Where were they? Who were they in their own minds? One woman almost ninety wanted desperately to get out the emergency exit because her father awaited her outside to drop her off at the school dance.

It was not fair to generalize about those individuals. She shuddered at the thought of identifying with the several residents who showed signs of Alzheimer's. Yet with great admiration she thought of President Reagan who had bravely announced his upcoming bout with "the long good bye." And Sergeant Shiver whose family faced the same events with the dreaded disease.

Both were bright and powerful men beloved by family who were just as powerless to combat the same fate as several of the center's residents. The specialized unit in this care center had closed and select individuals were chosen to be placed in the general population. Several residents were disturbed by their presence, but in varying degrees.

She rushed to her computer to search Alzheimer's Association. She needed to learn more. Down the hall came the raucous voice of a blind resident who must be in her 90's. "Mommy, Mommy. I didn't know. I didn't know. Cold, cold. Where are you? Where am I?" Then she went off into an undescribable wailing sound as if she were being chased by something. Alerted by the noise, an aide came in to call her by name and touch her to let her know of her presence. Quiet in the night at last! What is the answer? Is there one?

The spin-off by having residents with Alzheimer's is the tendency to spread a blanket over all residents as if everyone was afflicted with the same ailment, no matter what level of alertness that person might have. Labels are tricky, misleading and unfair. Then she decided that clinical facts were not what she needed, but recognition of the real people behind the label.

An uninvited visitor appeared suddenly in her room wheeling her chair toward the television set She called her name and said, "Your room is down the hall." But the visitor kept coming forward. The resident was in her recliner and could not reach her visitor who kept coming forward into the room beyond her reach. Her visitor reached down and snagged her mail basket by the handle.

"Here it is!" she declared as if she had been asked to find the treasure for her.

"Thanks, but you need to go back. Your room is down the hall." She turned around to exit, but in the process she caught the wheels of her chair on the wheeled bedside table and started dragging it toward the door. She was in danger of crashing into the computer.

The resident had pushed the call button to alert her aide of the unwanted visitor's presence so she could come to the rescue. She called out "Hey" very loudly for help as the table and visitor headed to be wedged in the doorway.

The visitor snapped back, "Shut up." The sad thing was that she knew her visitor and yet the visitor showed no signs of recognition of the other resident. "Where did my friend go?" she thought. She learned that her husband was no longer remembered either. Lost.

"Yipppeee! All day everyday! Up and down, Up and down! So good!" For hours on end with an occasional wordless tune sprinkled in or a hearty laugh, she went on and on. Or she was just as likely to say, "I want to go home. I can't be here. I want to go home." Repeatedly,. She was brought down to the dining room for meals with which she required help. Then it was back to the spot near the nursing station where residents requiring close supervision sat. Then back to her room for a nap.

A very loud demanding voice bellowed out. "Help me! God help me! I am a human being doesn't anyone care?" An aide had just left her room after giving her assistance. "It hurts. Why doesn't someone just call my daughter or is that too simple?" She had been given the maximum level of medication prescribed. She was abusive, calling people, aides, nurses, residents alike, vile names. She spit in the nurse's face and slapped her. She had called out accusingly from across the hall, looking in on her at the computer. "You know where my son is."

When she had answered "No," she was accused, "You are such a liar!" Was this person even in the right facility? she wondered. What right had she to judge such matters except her ears and nerves demanded it. She prayed that the woman would be quiet and then she thought perhaps a more appropriate prayer was that the woman feel no pain, just peace. Reports were that she was a perfect angel and very quiet and polite when her family members were present and then all hell broke loose when they left the building. She observed that she was quiet and attentive during the church service. Being lost manifests itself in many different ways. One resident taps her feet to the church music and uses she fingers to play an imaginary keyboard on her knees. She does not make a sound.

Hope

"Hope is the thing with feathers/ Which perches in the soul/ And sings the tune without the words/ And never stops at all!" This quotation from Emily Dickinson's poetry, encouraged her heart and buoyed her spirit each time she thought of it. She remembered her Mother saying "Live in hope or die in despair." Some people all around her seemed to represent those in struggle and sadness fighting off depression. Wishing tablemates a great day seemed a step in the right direction each morning. Corinthians declares that "Now remains faith, hope and charity (love) these three, but the greatest of these is love." To her there was no coincidence that Hope is the anchor of the three attributes. Her determination to "brighten the corner where you are" seemed an honorable directive from the lyrics of an old hymn. Encouraging herself was a beginning. Preparation for each day! Some days did not make that easy. Pain, personal and observed, gave rise to discouragement. But she determined to take it as a challenge for the day, maybe even for every day, but one day at a time. Another of her Mother's remarks grasped her: "Remember you are the only Bible some people will ever read."

Responsibility builds hope. Is hope transmittable or is it a hidden and self-made attribute? What does hope have to do with encouragement? How does one keep tablemates from squabbling over a parking space for two walkers beside their table? Being entrenched in the same ways squashes hope of tranquility for all who are around. This is especially true when each party has the attitude, "I'm here world, give way." Diplomatic training is sometimes needed to have any hope for peace at the table. Well, Sunday manners helps, but that is sometimes in short supply. Some love crowds and frequent if not constant entertainment, while some hope for a nap right after their meal, others just want to be alone with a good book or a favorite television program, bingo or a rousing bowling game on the Wii.

Hope is individual and triggered by upbringing and habits. How does one find it? How does one embrace HOPE? What is Hope any way after your career days have ended? Hope is the next generation. It is grandchildren and their futures, their lives and hopes and dreams and future contributions. Hope is a college you believe in and a school you helped create. Hope is awaking in the morning refreshed. Live in hope or die in despair. What is Hope? Then she remembered something she had written when she first entered the Center this time which seemed to answer that question.

Sermon in Stereo

"What am I doing here?" I thought as the church service began with "Blessed Assurance", a clarinet solo. Oh, I was eager to attend church, but just not here. I was supposed to be in my own apartment instead of a care center. Selling my home and moving into a independent living retirement complex had been my choice, but now I did not qualify to return to that facility even in the assisted living status. How did that happen? This isn't what I had planned.

The mini-concert ended. Group singing of hymns encouraged residents to join in as others were still being brought into the lobby beside the fireplace. Although I came early, I chose to sit toward the back of the room. On either side were residents I had known briefly, a man who wanders the halls constantly in his wheelchair and who has been in the center for 9 years, a woman who was recovering from knee replacement surgery and would be here only until she had completed physical therapy, another woman who had attended the sponsoring church before becoming a resident of the center, someone I saw frequently in the dining room and spoke to each morning, familiar faces, but basically strangers.

The speaker came to the podium and began a message of encouragement, a "Good Shepherd" talk. He spoke softly of loving care and warm feelings from a loving God. It was then staff wheeled in another resident who started speaking loudly in a rough voice, calling out urgently, "Hank, where are you? You promised never to leave me and here I am all alone. Where are you?" She said it repeatedly --again and AGAIN. I was sorely tempted to shush her, although I wasn't sure she was in any shape to hear anyone. So insistent, loud and annoying was this voice that not only did she drown out the speaker, it made me wonder why they even bothered to bring her to the service. This is stupid!

From somewhere inside my head a voice repeated a scripture I had not thought of in months. It said "when saw we Thee sick and ministered unto Thee? And the Lord answered, 'in as much as you did it unto the least of these, my brethren, you have done it unto Me.'"

Then one of the first Bible verses I ever memorized as a tiny child in a brush arbor came to me. "Be ye kind!"

Almost involuntarily my arm reached out to that resident in the wheelchair next to me. I said, "Will I do until Hank gets here?

She did not move or speak, but she was quiet, calm.

LaVergne, TN USA
16 February 2010
173243LV00001B/22/P